LAW OF TORTS

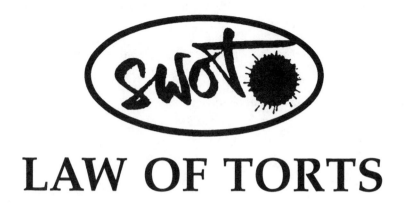

LAW OF TORTS

Fourth Edition

Peter Clark, LLB

Principal Lecturer in Law, University of Central Lancashire

Graham Stephenson, LLM, Solicitor

Principal Lecturer in Law, University of Central Lancashire

Series Editor: C.J. Carr, MA, BCL

BLACKSTONE
PRESS LIMITED

This edition published in Great Britain 1995 by Blackstone Press Limited, 9-15 Aldine Street, London W12 8AW. Telephone: 0181-740 1173

Previously published by Financial Training Publications Limited

First edition, 1985
Reprinted 1987
Reprinted 1988
Second edition, 1989
Reprinted 1991
Third edition, 1991
Fourth edition, 1995

ISBN: 1 85431 343 6

British Cataloguing in Publication Data
A CIP catalogue record for this book is available from the British Library

Typeset by Montage Studios Limited, Tonbridge, Kent
Printed by Bell & Bain Limited, Glasgow

CONTENTS

PREFACE

As we remarked in the preface to the third edition, we were awaiting the outcome of the litigation stemming from the Hillsborough disaster. As a result of the House of Lords' decision in *Alcock* v *Chief Constable of South Yorkshire*, there has been a substantial re-writing of the chapter on nervous shock, taking in also the relevant case of *McFarlane* v *E.E Caledonian*. Other chapters have, in the main, minor alterations only, the most important of which are probably the inclusion of the *Cambridge Water* case in the *Nuisance and Rylands* v *Fletcher* chapter, and *White* v *Jones*, HL (*Times* report only) in the Economic loss chapter although full certification of this case has not been possible.

We have introduced in line with other authors, a selected reading list at the end of each of the substantive law chapters and a bibliography at the end of the book to assist the student further.

We have also amended the general comments on study, revision and examination techniques in chapters 1 and 2 to take into account the structural changes in higher education in the last few years, in particular the tendency of courses to be established on a modular and/or semester basis, together with the increasing emphasis on coursework assessment.

Peter Clark
Graham Stephenson
March 1995

TABLE OF CASES

INTRODUCTION

If you are reading this introduction in order to decide whether or not this book is worth the price on its cover, as you ought to be, the questions foremost in your mind will no doubt be: Precisely what is this book about? What benefit would I gain, if any, from its purchase? We shall attempt to answer briefly these questions.

We have assumed that as a law undergraduate your immediate objective is to achieve the best possible class of honours degree. An upper second class honours degree is now almost a prerequisite for entry into either branch of the legal profession. In order to achieve this requisite qualification, you will need to acquire a certain level of knowledge of numerous areas of law. But knowledge as to the legal rules is not by itself sufficient. In addition you need to acquire what are termed 'lawyer's skills'. These include analytical and reasoning abilities, particularly in relation to legal concepts, and the capacity to read cases so as to identify the material facts and extract the legal principles. These skills are particularly important to the study of tort law which is both heavily conceptual and a common law or case law subject. In other subjects, legislation may predominate and the student has to be able to cope with complex and often esoteric language of numerous statutory provisions.

The attainment of these qualities by the student is regarded as the sole objective of the learning programme. Lectures, tutorials (seminars) are almost exclusively devoted to that end — the acquisition of the lawyerly skills is an end in itself.

But what of the means to that end? A student of law must acquire those means. Other skills are needed here — study skills. Students have to learn how to study law efficiently, to gain maximum benefit from the three different learning situations — lectures, seminars and private study, which are common features of undergraduate courses.

Furthermore, a student needs to develop some fairly sophisticated communicative skills for, in order to achieve his goal of a good honours degree, he has to communicate his knowledge and understanding, demonstrate his analytical powers, through the somewhat peculiar medium of law assessment. The semesterisation of course units has led to a greater use of 'seen' or 'open book' assessment. But whatever the style of the assessment adopted, it is highly likely that the student's knowledge and reasoning abilities will be tested through the use of legal problems.

It is our experience that many students consistently underperform because they fail to develop sufficiently their study and communicative skills. We believe this results largely from the fact that in many institutions very little, if anything, is done in the way of providing students with effective guidance as to how to study law efficiently, present papers in seminars, and develop even a reasonable assessment technique. This book seeks, in a modest way, to provide that guidance and to help students to achieve assessment results which do not understate their abilities. It is important that students should appreciate that underperformance through poor examination technique may affect not only the student clinging to the pass mark by his finger-nails, but also those who obtain better results. A student who obtains a third-class mark may have been afflicted far less in this respect than a student who underachieves albeit with a higher-class mark.

HOW CAN THIS BOOK HELP STUDENTS?

First, a word of warning, reading the book of itself will do little to enhance a student's performance, that will only be achieved by the student giving diligent thought to, and being dedicated in the application of, the advice given.

In chapter 1, we have set out some basic guidance on study methods and the organisation of work. Chapter 2 contains a fairly detailed analysis of assessment technique, including some advice on revision. These chapters deal with quite a number of points which may be regarded as so obvious as not to require stating. This is not our experience: students quite commonly make some extremely elementary errors.

The rest of the book is devoted entirely to illustrating the application of assessment techniques by way of a series of questions on various topics within the law of torts. In this respect it has been necessary to be selective. Torts is a vast subject which is unlikely to be covered comprehensively in any teaching syllabus. The content of syllabuses will vary as between institutions. We have therefore tried to select those topics which are likely to be common to most if not all syllabuses. For each of these topics we have drawn attention to those aspects of the law which, for one reason or another, are likely to be found in assessment questions and with which students experience some degree of difficulty. Our treatment of the substantive law is therefore selective. This book is not intended as a textbook, nor will it satisfactorily serve as such.

In providing both guidance and explanation on points of technique as well as the substantive issues involved in the illustrative questions, we have deliberately avoided giving what might be termed as a 'model answer' or 'crib'. Such a format would have been impracticable for these purposes. Further, we recognise that there exists a variation in individual style and approach which is perfectly acceptable and we would not wish to create any contrary impression.

What we have attempted to do is to indicate with regard to each topic what are the difficult issues and to embody those issues, or at least some of them, in the questions. We have sought to do this in a fashion which will give students an insight into the *assessor's* technique — hopefully the book will reveal as much about that as it does about the technique of the student's response.

Our objectives have largely dictated the content of each chapter which is:

(a)   An outline of the substantive issues with which the student may find difficulty.
(b)   Sample assessment questions.
(c)   Notes explaining points of technique and the substantive issues raised in the questions.

We have not made the various defences available in the law of torts the subject of a separate chapter, but have incorporated them in the sample questions as appropriate. Each of the sample questions has been constructed so as to raise numerous substantive issues, consequently the explanatory notes may occasionally be quite lengthy. We have not felt the need to restrict the construction of the questions according to the constraints of examination conditions. The questions are rather exercises to be undertaken as you progress through the course when the amount of time taken is a far less pressing consideration.

The primary aim of this book is to enable students to improve their ability to deal with problem questions, whatever the style of the assessment which is employed. This cannot be done in or around the time of the assessment itself but, as we stress at various places in the first chapters, preparation for assessment starts from the moment your course starts. You should read chapters 1 and 2 right at the outset as we believe they contain useful information on study techniques and so on. Subsequent chapters can be looked at as and when your tutors consider the relevant topic in class. This will give you more experience of coping with problem-type questions. In the next two chapters we have sought to take account of the major changes in legal education which have taken place in recent times, in particular, the modularisation and semesterisation of course units, with the consequent refinement in methods of assessment.

1 STUDY TECHNIQUES

Most law degree courses are comprised of three quite different learning situations: lectures, private study and seminars or tutorials. In many but by no means all institutions, the schedule of seminars is planned to follow selectively in the footsteps of the programme of lectures in each subject, thus facilitating a three-stage progression in learning, the interim period being that which students devote to private study. Such a system will be new to most first-year students and makes demands of them other than in a purely academic sense. They have to learn how to learn within the system. In view of the volume of, and speed at which, information is hurled at them, students have to do so very quickly.

This problem is not confined to first-year students. Bad study habits acquired in the first year tend to be continued and affect the academic performance of students who are relatively successful in their finals. In the following pages we have sought to alert students to some of the more common pitfalls and to advise how students might learn more effectively in each of the three different situations.

LECTURES

We believe students will find it useful if we begin by stating the basic objectives of a lecture programme. With knowledge of these objectives a student will be in a better position to understand his own role in the lecture. In particular he should be better able to appreciate what information should be noted and have a clearer understanding of which information is the more important.

One objective of lectures is to convey to students a basic knowledge and understanding of the law itself. This, however, is perhaps a more complex operation than the new student will readily appreciate. In order to state what the law is, or is thought to be, the lecturer may well embark upon a close examination of case law and/or statutory provisions. Usually he will seek to explain how decided cases relate to each other and to stated principles, often tracing a twisted path through a number of cases and judgments.

Secondly, lectures provide important guidance to students so that they may more readily gain, in private study, a deeper understanding through an informed and selective approach to legal materials. Such guidance may be explicit, 'When you read this case note especially . . .'. The guidance may be less obvious, when, for example, the lecturer states in what appears to be a 'throwaway line', 'Contrast the views of Bloggs LJ in *Smith* v *Smith*'. The guiding hand may not be at all obvious, but merely implicit in the lecturer's selection of cases and judgments in much the same way that guidance may be found in the treatment of case law in textbooks. The more important cases are to be found in the text whilst many others of lesser import are confined to the footnotes.

But lectures are much more even than this. They represent a most important opportunity to stimulate the interest of students in the subject and to cultivate in them the spirit and practice of critical analysis. This may well be attempted by the lecturer seizing upon some difficult and/or controversial issue, challenging the student's intellect upon matters which the lecturer will often offer an opinion.

It is our experience that many students do not benefit as much as they might from lectures. This may well be due in part to the fact that they are not acquainted with these basic objectives and are therefore unclear as to what they ought to be doing in lectures. They are rightly concerned to make 'a good set of notes', but their view as to what amounts to such is frequently misconceived. Many students adopt a passive role in lectures, by which we mean that they take upon themselves the mantle of silent unthinking scribes, committed to capturing on paper every word uttered by the lecturer whether understood or not.

Whilst lectures are not a forum for discussion students can and should participate more actively in the sense of devoting more effort towards following the understanding and content of lectures and being far more selective in their note taking. Given this a student will be better able to ask a more meaningful question at the end of a lecture than 'What was the word after . . .?' Please do not misunderstand. We believe it is important that a student should create a good set of notes from which he will ultimately revise. The thing to recognise is that those notes should be built up in stages, lectures, private study and notes made in preparation for, or during, seminars. Notes taken in lectures should be regarded as the foundation upon which to build.

Viewed in this way a more sensible perspective will be gained as to what and how much should be noted in lectures themselves.

In a number of institutions lecturers have sought to alleviate student difficulty in this respect by the use of lecture 'hand-outs', which contain a summary of the essential points of a lecture, case references etc. In many institutions such a simple and basic innovation remains unemployed. The following advice is offered on the assumption that the latter situation appertains and that you are expected to make notes whilst your lecturer is in full flight. In general terms the purpose of that advice is to try to ensure that only the most relevant information is recorded in lectures in a manner which will enable greater concentration upon the content of the lecture, thus providing a more informed approach to private study and facilitating additional note making at that stage. In view of the fact that the law of torts is very much a case law subject we have oriented the guidance towards the question:

What are the Important Points to Note about Cases?

First, students need to assess the individual lecturer. Lecturers vary in their approach from the exceedingly detailed and technical treatment of cases on the one hand, to the 'overview'style on the other. Where the latter approach is adopted, a lecture may take the form of a commentary upon development in the law in general or doctrinal terms with no mention whatever of the details of any particular decision. Where this approach is employed the lecturer may well expect that a basic knowledge and understanding of the subject-matter has been acquired through prior reading of textbooks, cases etc.

Most lecturers fall between these extremes but nevertheless demonstrate a degree of variation in approach which needs to be recognised and may result in a different method of taking notes from different lecturers. Generally, the more unselective the lecturer the more selective the notes taken by students and vice versa. Below are the essential points upon which a student should make clear and concise notes. We have assumed that the student understands the common law doctrine of precedent.

(a)   The stated principle in relation to which cases are to be considered.

(b)   The *ratio* of any case as indicated by the lecturer, i.e., the material facts together with the decision thereon. If the lecturer confines himself to stating only the material facts a précis of those facts should be made and usually this need occupy no more than a couple of lines. In the event that a lecturer over indulges in factual detail (most of us are guilty of this at some time) the student should be guided by his common sense and the experience he acquires. When reading cases at a later stage notes on facts may be embellished. Try to ensure at that stage that the facts noted are both necessary and sufficient to the proposition of law said to be stated in the case.

(c) Any *obiter* statements to which the lecturer refers should be noted. Though such statements are said to be only of persuasive authority their impact upon the subsequent development of the law may well be far greater than the *ratio* of the case in question, especially in decisions of the House of Lords or even the Court of Appeal. Obvious examples of this would include Lord Atkin's statement of the so called 'neighbour' principle in *Donoghue* v *Stevenson* [1932] AC 562 at 580. Much of what the House of Lords had to say concerning the duty of care not to give negligent advice in *Hedley Byrne & Co. Ltd* v *Heller & Partners Ltd* [1964] AC 465 was also technically *obiter*. Yet both have been of fundamental importance in the subsequent development of the tort of negligence. Other less prestigious *obiter* statements may well be referred to by your lecturer. Clearly he regards them as being of some importance and so should you by noting them albeit as *obiter* statements.

(d) As to the lecturer's evaluation of cases under review especially noteworthy are his observations on:

(i) How the decision in any particular case relates to the stated principle and to the decisions in other cases. Did the decision in *Smith* v *Smith* appear to widen or narrow the principle? Was some previous case distinguished, followed or overruled?

(ii) The insight which the decision gives into some legal concept. For example moral blameworthiness would seem to be strongly implicit in the layman's understanding of negligent conduct. But what of the 'legal' concept of negligence. Consider the implications of the decisions in *Nettleship* v *Weston* [1971] 2 QB 691 and *Roberts* v *Ramsbottom* [1980] 1 All ER 7 which support the view that a person may be negligent at law without moral obloquy.

(iii) The considerations underlying the formulation of the statement of law in any particular case. The case of *Nettlesbip* v *Weston* affords a convenient illustration in which Megaw LJ took the view that the standard of care in the tort of negligence was to be objectively assessed, creating a single hypothetical standard with which all persons had to comply. The defendant learner-driver in that case was required to meet the standard of a competent qualified driver. In the course of his judgment Megaw LJ indicates quite clearly why he took that view. It was his concern as to the uncertainty which would be created in the law by the introduction of a doctrine of variable standards.

(e) Where full references to cases are given in lectures, e.g., *Dredger Liesbosch (Owners)* v *SS Edison (Owners)* [1933] AC 449 HL, students will no doubt wish to record them in full. However, you should not allow yourself to be distracted if you fail to catch every detail of the case reference. The case name is important and, in the context of the lecture itself, the court in which it was decided, House of Lords, Court of Appeal etc. Do make a point of checking and correcting case names as necessary at a later stage. The incorrect spelling of a case name may well give the examiner the impression that you have not read the case in question. Other information in the reference, i.e., the title, year, volume and page reference in the reports is useful but not vital at this stage, as are the page references to particular points in judgments. Noting this information accurately can save valuable time later.

There are certain other matters concerning the content of lecture notes to which a student should give particular consideration. Below we advise students to use headings and subheadings when taking notes. On balance we regard this as a helpful and sensible way of recording information. Any such system of compartmentalising information does not, however, promote one's ability to perceive how the constituent parts of any particular tort interrelate or indeed enable one to gain an overall perspective upon the tort as a whole.

A similar problem occurs at quite a different level in the law of torts which is largely made up of a number of nominate and innominate torts. Though general trends are clearly discernible across the boundaries of these torts there are arguably sufficient differences in the rules applicable to each of them to justify separate and individual treatment. Whether your lecturer chooses to approach the subject-matter via general trends or through specific individual torts is a matter of his personal preference. The former approach tends to emphasise similarities as between the various torts, whilst the latter approach tends to emphasise the distinctions which exist between them. Such differences of approach can be found in the established student textbooks. Compare for example the different ways in which the subject matter is ordered in Street on Torts and Winfield and Jolowicz on Tort. The lecturer's choice of recommended textbook may give an indication as to which approach he has chosen to adopt.

Whichever approach is adopted it is fair to say that many examination questions may require a student to demonstrate a knowledge and under-standing of either an individual tort or the distinctions and common elements of different torts. We shall pursue this matter further in the chapter on examination technique. For the present it is important that students recognise that guidance is given in the course of lectures with respect to both of the above-mentioned matters. Forewarned is forearmed, students should listen carefully for and note such guidance as is given in this respect. This is a matter of substantial importance to the student's understanding of the law of torts, the investment of time and effort in subsequent study is likely to pay handsome dividends.

Not every point made by the lecturer will be fully understood at the time. Quite often the student himself is aware that he has not fully understood and it is a sensible practice to physically emphasise in your notes any such points.

You should make every attempt to resolve any such misunderstandings either through questions to your lecturer or tutor if the opportunity arises, or through your own efforts. Your lecturer or seminar tutor will usually be the person who sets your examination. He knows through experience the issues with which students have difficulty. You will appreciate that it is no accident therefore that many of those issues which students never quite understand are to be found in examination/coursework questions.

Note Form

Students would also be well advised to give some thought to the following points as to the form in which they make notes:

(a)   Bearing in mind the advice given above, use and physically emphasise headings and sub-headings as appropriate and in general be generous in terms of the spacing of notes. These twin practices are in our view beneficial for a number of reasons. The generous spacing allows for complementary detail to be added at a later stage without having to rewrite the whole of one's notes. The headings and sub-headings provide structure and create an obvious skeletal framework of the topic covered. This promotes clarity and enables the material to be more easily ingested. Students will find this of considerable assistance when revising, for revision inevitably involves a process of distillation.

(b)   We would advise students to maintain a reasonable standard of neatness and legibility. We suspect that many students take the view that it is sufficient if they themselves can read and follow their notes as and when required. The danger which lies in the habit of writing in this subjective fashion is the likely production under pressure in the examination of an illegible script. It is probably true to say that nothing exasperates an examiner more than this. Do not on any account fall into the trap of taking 'mayfly' notes, i.e., notes scribbled in such a fashion that they have to be rewritten afterwards in relative leisure. The remedial effort must be made in lectures if legibility is to be maintained under pressure in the examination.

(c)   Whilst the maintenance of legibility in note taking may well prove valuable in examinations, the same cannot be said of any system of abbreviation which a student might adopt. Abbreviation is a time-saving device to be employed essentially in lectures. Some limited abbreviation is acceptable in examination, e.g., P = plaintiff, D = defendant, or the names of parties involved may be signified by the appropriate initial. In examinations a student should not go beyond this general boundary except where absolutely necessary where perhaps he has allowed himself insufficient time to write a full answer to his final question. So far as lecture notes are concerned a system of abbreviation can be carried much further so long as the student understands his own system. In the course of a single lecture various words and phrases are used with almost monotonous frequency. In a lecture on the tort of negligence the terms reasonable foresight, reasonably foreseeable, reasonable care will abound. We would think it not beyond the wit of students to abbreviate these and many other such terms.

(d) We see the use of précis as being quite separate from that of abbreviation outlined above. Simply put it is the art of capturing in fewer words the essential point of a larger statement. Many students make absolutely no attempt to summarise the lecturer's statements, as each word falls from the lecturer's lips it appears at the end of their pens producing page after page of undistinguished, unselective notes. We believe that the practice of succinctly recording what the lecturer has to say, as far as possible in the student's own words, is enormously important. It is not simply that the amount that is written is reduced, but it orders the student's involvement in the lecture to listening, thinking, then writing selectively and briefly and that is how we believe it should be.

SEMINARS AND TUTORIALS

Seminars and tutorials perform an important function in any degree programme and should be given considerable attention both with regard to preparation beforehand and contribution during class. Class contact is at a premium in most institutions of higher education and far too many students do not put what little they have to good use. We propose to say something about both aspects of seminar work, but a lot of what we say in the following chapter on private study has a bearing on the way you should prepare for seminars.

Seminars should ideally be a dialogue between *all* those involved. It is your opportunity to show your understanding of the subject under discussion, to clarify any misconceptions and, most importantly, to air your views and have them tested by your tutor and your fellow students. This is an opportunity which unfortunately many students spurn.

Preparation

Preparation for seminars or tutorials is essential if you are to play your part in the discussion in class. Some students, however, for one reason or another do not prepare at all but nonetheless attend. Our view is that they may as well be in the library catching up on the work they have omitted to do. Other students' perceptions of what is involved in preparation vary somewhat, from those who merely bring their lecture notes along and try to answer questions while leafing through them, to those who do virtually all the reading but fail to spend any time considering the questions set for group discussion. These variants and all in between are unsatisfactory and the student is failing to use the opportunities given by class contact hours.

You must attempt to read as much of the material listed as possible. How much of it you do will depend upon your capacity for absorbing material, and we shall make some further comments shortly in the section on private study on how to cope with cases, textbooks, articles and other reading matter.

In our experience we have found that the majority of students have done enough preparation in the sense of having read a substantial amount of material. However, the major shortcoming in seminar preparation is the failure to apply the knowledge gathered in the reading to the problems or essays set for discussion. Time and again students come to seminars or tutorials with little idea how to tackle the problem under discussion. Our experience shows that ability to answer such questions, rather than lack of knowledge is a persistent factor in student failure to achieve their potential. If students were to think more about the problems set for seminar work, there is every chance that their technique would improve and consequently their coursework and examination performance. It must be stressed that we are not suggesting a full written answer to seminar problems (unless this has been specified by the tutor) but that you should try to answer the problem in note form for easy use during class discussion. An additional bonus may well be that it is common practice for tutors to use past examination questions as a basis for class discussion. The benefit of adequate preparation before the seminar should be obvious and will no doubt result in an improved technique when examination time comes round.

Seminar Contribution

There are many different ways to conduct a seminar but what should occur, as we have said before, is a dialogue between all concerned. It is all very well doing a large amount of preparation for a seminar merely to turn up and remain mute throughout the proceedings. Unfortunately, too many students, for whatever reason, are prepared to allow the burden of discussion to fall on the few, usually the tutor and one or two others. There is a tendency to treat a seminar as just another note-taking session. Notes can be taken but only sparingly when, perhaps, a point you had not thought about crops up. The tutor may emphasise a particular issue, then it may be justifiable to note it. Otherwise, the emphasis in seminars should be on discussion. You should be prepared to contribute not just factual information but also to make points of an evaluative nature. For example, if you take the view that the courts discriminate too heavily in favour of plaintiffs in road traffic accidents as opposed to injuries sustained in surgical operations, then you should be prepared to say so and argue your case. Your views may be fairly uninformed at an early stage in your legal studies, but nonetheless you should attempt to take up a tenable position.

Whatever career you eventually choose following your degree studies, oral as well as written skills will generally be essential. Seminars are the appropriate place in which to develop such skills. In any event, if your seminars are assessed it will be vital to improve these skills.

One final point on this topic is to remind you to collect together your lecture notes, as amplified and clarified, and the notes made for and during the seminar into a coherent whole. This will be of immense value when you come to examination revision. You can ill afford time just before the examination in compiling and rationalising various sets of notes on individual topics.

PRIVATE STUDY

Very few people are capable of passing a torts examination or coursework by merely attending lectures and seminars without in addition doing a substantial amount of private study. This aspect of your degree studies is probably the most crucial. One or two students may succeed by doing very little during the academic year or semester and then doing a revision crash course, but inevitably their marks will be a lot lower than they otherwise would have been. Indeed, such students are often on the borderline between pass and fail completely. Degree-level studies should be regarded as a learning rather than a teaching exercise and great emphasis is placed in this book on the need for a large measure of private study on your part. We shall make some comments on the amount of time which should or might be spent on this aspect of your studies and also make some suggestions as to how that time might usefully be employed. Naturally, how much time you are prepared to devote may depend on other interests and/or the capacity of any particular individual to assimilate and absorb materials and what we say can only be by way of general guidance. Semesterisation brings with it even greater pressures which necesitate better organisation and time arrangement.

How Much Time?

No hard and fast rule can be given for the reason expressed in the previous comment but you may find some of the following points useful:

(a) It is essential that you establish some sort of routine; whether you stick to it rigidly or not does not matter, as long as it can be maintained more or less.

(b) Get into the good habit of trying to work between classes, even if there is only an hour available. You could perhaps read a couple of cases or a short chapter in your textbook in that time.

(c) You should be prepared to work for at least three evenings per week until the library closes. This may result in your having your weekends completely free for relaxation, sport or other leisure interests. These are also important aspects of studies. You *must* take some time off — how much is a matter for each individual.

(d)   If your library opens on Saturdays, then you should try to use this time for finding those cases, articles or other materials which you could not find during the week. Pressure on available resources is increasing and you are much more likely to obtain popular materials on a Saturday.

(e)   Do not work too late in the evening. You should rarely work after 9 p.m. as your mind is less receptive the later you work. It is better to go to bed early and get up early in order to work. You can probably achieve more in an hour before breakfast than you can in a late evening session. Also shorter spells of work are generally more productive in terms of assimilation of material, as concentration lapses the longer you are studying in any one spell.

What To Do In the Time?

From what has already been said in the parts on lectures and seminars you should have gathered to some extent what you should be doing during private study. For the sake of emphasis we consider you should be doing the following:

(a)   Amplifying and clarifying lectures on a topic, including reading of cases, textbooks and recommended articles.

(b)   Seminar preparation, some or all of which may overlap with (a) but *remember* to attempt answers to seminar problems as already mentioned.

(c)   Course work, whether assessed or not, is worth doing well. Effort put into essays, if not themselves assessed, is usually repaid with a bonus at examination time, particularly where the topic of the essay reappears in some form in the examination, a common occurrence in our experience.

Technique

We propose to take a closer look at the reading materials you have been recommended and we have a few suggestions to make as to how you go about your task of reading and note taking. Your reading list on torts will no doubt contain references to what seems to be an abundance of cases, textbooks, articles of one kind or another and occasionally reports by Government departments or bodies such as the Law Commission. At first sight this may be off-putting, particularly since tutors in other subjects will be giving you comparable lists on the apparent assumption that their course is the only one you are doing and you have unlimited time to pursue the finer points.

The best advice we can give you is not to be put off, do not despair and become frustrated. If you have established a routine of working and follow some of our suggestions below, the reading lists should become manageable.

You may still not be able to read everything on every reading list. Few students can achieve this, but you should aim to do a substantial amount, so that you can say something useful in tutorials.

Cases

The aim in reading case reports is to extract exactly what you need with a minimum of effort. Good casebooks will do this for you, although it must be remembered that any such book will reflect in the extracts selected, the choice made by the persons who compiled it. In addition, it may be slightly out of date and you will still need to read the latest case reports. The student who does not have ready access to a law library or those who prefer to work at home may well find casebooks useful and convenient. Part-time students, particularly, are recommended to obtain good casebooks.

For those who cannot, or do not use casebooks, there is obviously more work involved until one develops with experience a technique for getting to the crux of any case. In your introduction to the legal system course, whatever it is called, you will be introduced to *ratio decidendi, obiter dicta* and so on, so we do not propose to discuss them in this context. Below are a few practical points which in our experience should prove useful and time-saving.

(a) Read the headnote which will normally be an accurate reproduction of the facts and the decision.

(b) The reporter himself may well refer you to the important parts of any particular judge's speech. This will enable you to go immediately to the relevant part of the judgment. In some instances this should suffice and it will not be necessary to read the whole or all of the judgments. Certainly, however, in leading cases you should read the judgments and see the way each judge approaches the legal issue involved. At the outset of your studies reading judgments in full may be no bad thing in itself, although time may well be a factor. You should be guided, where appropriate, by your tutor's or lecturer's comments. The reading of judgments may also provide a spin-off in the sense that the exercise may well help you to acquire a style to be adopted in your own legal arguments.

(c) As far as note taking of cases is concerned, if you adopt a card-index system then this will ensure you do not take too many notes and that those you do take are concise. What you need is a brief statement of facts, the decision preferably in your own words and any important statements by a judge. In leading cases, you may wish to have a note of the differing approaches, if such be the case, of the judges. So, for example, in the case of *Hedley Byrne & Co. Ltd* v *Heller & Partners Ltd* [1964] AC 465, you may wish to make a note of the various ways in which the judges described the specially close relationship required before a duty of care may arise in respect of a negligent misstatement. Generally speaking, leading cases will be those in the

Court of Appeal and the House of Lords but remember some High Court decisions are important, for example *Ross* v *Caunters* [1980] Ch 297 and *Yianni* v *Edwin Evans & Sons* [1982] QB 438, the authority of which has now been confirmed by the Court of Appeal and House of Lords respectively (see *White* v *Jones* [1993] 3 All ER 481, (1995) *The Times*, 17 February and *Smith* v *Bush* [1989] 3 All ER 514).

(d)   In those series of reports where the arguments of counsel are set out, it will normally not be necessary to read them. Nonetheless, it is occasionally good practice to read counsel's arguments, particularly if you are interested in mooting, as it may well give you some hints on how to prepare and submit a legal argument.

(e)   Dissenting judgments should also be considered, as they may provide useful ammunition in future cases for arguing that a decision was wrong or is capable of being distinguished or that the position is not really settled beyond doubt. The case of *Mutual Life & Citizens' Assurance Co. Ltd* v *Evatt* [1971] AC 793, a Privy Council case, shows the value to be attributed to a dissenting speech (of itself unusual in Privy Council cases).

Textbooks
Textbooks in the main should be read with a view to clarifying ambiguities and difficulties in lecture notes and for purposes of amplification on points referred to in lectures. This may, however, depend on the lecturer's technique — if he or she is taking the overview approach you may have to make substantial notes from your recommended text. Again, it is worth emphasising that too many notes can cause problems at revision and examination time. It should not normally be necessary for you to follow up references in footnotes or elsewhere in your textbook, unless either this course of action is suggested by the lecturer on a particular point, or you are researching a point for course work or tutorials. Material in footnotes is likely to be less important, the main material being included in the text. Also a further word of warning needs to be given. Textbook writers tend to allude to every possible case or other reference, even where the case does not take the principle of law any further, but is merely an example of its application. It is important to remember that cases are examples of principles or propositions of law, and normally one or two cases only are required to show how the principle works. The excessive citation of cases in indiscriminate fashion is to be discouraged.

Articles and reports
Nowadays, there is a wide range of materials available to which students are referred. These include learned articles in a whole variety of journals published worldwide, and reports by the Law Commission, Royal Commissions, Government departments and so on. There is a wealth of material,

some of which is of great value to students of torts. It can be off-putting and again we must emphasise that too many notes on items in these various sources is not desirable.

Articles

The scope of articles in legal journals varies. Some are fairly descriptive of case law or recent statutes, others will be an attempt to be critical and say something original or enlightening on a particular topic. All have their uses. There is little point in making detailed notes on an article at the outset. You should read it through to gather a general impression of the writer's argument. It may well be that the article has been given to you, not with a view to its detailed argument on any point, but with regard to the general point (if any) being made by the writer. It may well be merely this aspect which you need to note and nothing more. The writer may be critical of the approach taken in a series of cases or in recent legislation. He may be trying to establish a trend from a series of cases. For example, in 1971 there was published in the *Modern Law Review* an article by C.R. Symmons entitled 'The duty of care in negligence: recently expressed policy elements' (34 MLR 394, 528), in which the writer explored some recent negligence cases, particularly *Home Office* v *Dorset Yacht Co. Ltd* [1970] AC 1004 and attempted an analysis which indicated the judicial trend in such cases. The article emphasises the point that there has developed a tendency for judges to clearly express the judicial policy behind decisions in negligence cases. It may well be that your lecturer, in citing this article, wishes you to grasp this main, essential point, although reading the article in full will inevitably improve your understanding of the cases and the points he discusses. It may be unnecessary to take detailed notes on such an article, and in most cases the taking of such notes is to be avoided. A more recent article in similar vein is that by Smith and Burns entitled *'Donoghue* v *Stevenson*: The not so golden anniversary', which is to be found in (1983) 46 MLR 147. In that article the authors criticise the judgment of Lord Wilberforce in *Anns* v *Merton London Borough Council* [1977] 2 All ER 492, HL, to the extent that Lord Wilberforce appears to disregard the fundamental distinction between misfeasance and nonfeasance which is firmly established in the law of torts. A student would be well advised to read this article and consider very carefully how much he really needs to extract from it. Some of the sentiments expressed in this article have certainly found favour in subsequent cases which has led to a departure from the approach taken by Lord Wilberforce in *Anns* (see, in particular, *Murphy* v *Brentwood* [1990] 2 All ER 908, HL).

Reports

Law Commission working papers and reports are an extremely useful source both of the then existing legal rules and proposals for reform. A student may obtain an extremely good critique of existing law in such a document and also from the reform proposals develop a critical attitude towards the material. Likewise, a Royal Commission Report — and the one that springs to mind immediately is that known as the Pearson Commission Report on Civil Liability and Compensation for Personal Injury (Cmnd 7054) in 1978. Whilst few of the proposals in that report have been enacted and the report may appear a little dated, there is a vast amount of important critical and informative material which a student can still make use of. However, note taking should be kept to a minimum: you should attempt to précis the proposals and any conclusions drawn by the authors in such materials. Quite often, reports, and for that matter articles, will contain useful material for course work, in particular apposite quotations or statements which can be used to support your argument. You should, therefore, be on the look-out for useful phrases and make a note of them or where they can be found. This applies generally.

CONCLUSION

Private study, it needs repeating, is probably the most crucial aspect of your studies. The amount of study and the way you go about studying on your own will in nearly every case have an impact on whether you pass or fail, or obtain a third or a lower second and so on. Ultimately, however, overall success depends on how well, during the year/semester at least, you combine private study with your class contact in the form of lectures and seminars or tutorials.

2   REVISION AND ASSESSMENT TECHNIQUES

REVISION

Revision time can be a soul-destroying period but you can make things easier for yourself by following some of the advice below. However, it is worth repeating the point that how you go about this will vary with each individual. Some prefer to mix with their fellow sufferers, to others this is something to be avoided at all costs. Wherever and however you revise, you should ensure that you take sufficient time for relaxation and you do not work too late in the evening or for *long* spells. Revision periods may be considerably reduced as a consequence of semesterisation.

(a)   The first point is a reminder that good preparation during the academic year semester will save a lot of heartache when it comes to revision. During the last few weeks running up to the examination period, the last thing you want is to be preparing notes on a topic for the first time. This work should have been done steadily over the previous months.

(b)   Routine is once again an important factor. You should plan your weeks and days, so that revision work becomes a habit, but not an unthinking habit.

(c)   Assuming that you have done your preparation during the year, you should have a series of separate and identifiable topics within the subject area of torts. As has already been mentioned, it is dangerous to compartmentalise materials in this way without remaining aware of the interconnection between the various topics. Nonetheless, it is still a useful and probably essential way to proceed. It may be that at this stage you can clearly identify several topics which might justify a full examination question. Factors which will be a good indication of whether a topic may be examined upon will include whether a seminar was devoted to the topic and the types of questions set in past examination papers. This latter source is probably the most fruitful in terms of enabling you to assess the likelihood of questions on particular topics. Attempting answers to past examination papers at this stage is a useful way of assessing the effectiveness of your revision.

(d)   If you are not fortunate to be in that small minority of people who have the ability to revise every topic and, consequently, be in a position to answer every question on an examination paper, then it is better to be realistic and be selective in the number of topics you revise. If the examination allows you a choice of four or five out of nine or ten questions set, then it may for many people be a wasted effort to find yourself embarrassed for choice in your torts examination, and as a result not spend enough time on your other subjects. It makes sense to select, say, at least six topics and possibly seven which you consider likely to appear in some shape or form on the examination paper. You need some margin of error, just in case a favourite examiner's topic is omitted from the paper. In addition, even if your forecast is right and questions on your five main topics appear as expected, it is possible that a question set may be particularly difficult. If you have revised one or two reserve topics, you may be able to avoid a difficult question. Whatever the range of choice on any particular paper, the principle is the same.

(e)   The material you should be revising from should ideally be that compiled on your own together with lecture and tutorial handouts, lecture notes, notes on articles, reports and cases collected during the year. It is unwise to attempt revision from textbooks, articles and reports themselves. You will find it much easier to recall information that you have written yourself. Reading from textbooks and so on may well be unproductive and far too time-consuming at this stage of the academic year when time is of the essence.

(f)   We do not propose to give very specific advice on how to organise your entire revision programme but some points are worth emphasis. You should not concentrate on any one subject to the detriment of others. There may be a temptation to do this if you feel particularly weak in say torts or contract. The subject studied first will suffer considerably if you have no time to refresh your memory on it. A more suitable way of approaching this problem might be to spend initially a short period on each subject and then as the material becomes more familiar, progressively less time as the examination period approaches. The more often you read through material the better will be your understanding of it and your ability to recall information. We would not recommend rote learning as a rule but some students feel happier with this technique and that is entirely up to them. We would, however, advise students to learn off by heart some basic definitions, for example those of assault or battery. You may if you wish construct your own definitions which embrace all the elements of other torts. These can be relatively easily constructed using headings and subheadings from your notes. Any such suggestion may well be controversial and deserves explanation.

When a student is confronted with a problem question his first task is to identify a significant number of specific issues involved. When the facts of the problem are searched against a definition he is likely to recognise more of those issues than would otherwise be the case. In a sense the definition tells the student to some extent what he ought to be looking for in the facts of the problem.

In advocating the use of this technique in this limited way it should not be thought that we are encouraging parrot-like regurgitation, or simplistic thinking. The use of definitions as a 'teaching aid' should be 'temporary'. Whilst they enable the student to see the 'wood for the trees', they should be given with the caveat that, in the light of the knowledge the student subsequently acquires, he should recognise definitions as the oversimplifications which they often are. We have already warned of the compartmentalising effect of using headings and subheadings. Students should not allow definitions to bridle or blinker their understanding of the subject. There is no reason why their use as an *aide-memoire* should have that effect.

Students often delude themselves about their lack of ability to recall material. Most have little confidence in their mental powers at some stage and their fears are often unfounded.

(g) As the examinations approach you should only attempt to read the material through in a relaxed manner. By this time you should be as familiar with it as you could possibly be and you should slacken off the intensity of concentration a little. The last day or two before the examinations should be fairly relaxed. There is little use cramming and working all hours possible. This approach is as likely to be counter-productive as anything else. Some advise that you should do no work at all the day before an examination, but if you feel the need to do something, a quick glance through your notes on one or two of the more difficult topics you have chosen will probably be all that is necessary.

(h) Any time between examinations can be used productively, but unless the gap is at least a fortnight between two exams, it is extremely unwise to leave your entire revision of a whole subject to that period. You should be merely consolidating and refreshing your memory during such gaps.

(i) Revision should ideally be a process of distillation. It should be the time when your year's work comes to fruition — not when it starts.

EXAMINATION TECHNIQUE

The moment towards which all the semester/year's work has been geared arrives all too quickly for most people, not least examiners who have the unenviable task of marking a vast number of papers. Before making some specific points about what you should or should not do once you are sitting at your desk, a couple of general comforting points. First, the examiner wants you to pass — he is not trying to catch you out. You are being provided with the opportunity to show that you can assimilate and understand material and apply it to given situations. Secondly, if you have followed most of the advice given earlier in this book, then you should be able to approach your torts examination with a lot less dread and you may even enjoy it. Whether you enjoy it or not your year's hard work should stand you in good stead. What you must not do is throw all that away by doing something stupid once in the examination room. Time and again we have seen students throw away the chance of a good examination mark because they fail to observe one or more of the points below. This may say something about the all-or-nothing nature of the examination system and its pressures. It also often says something about the student. Preparation for your examination starts at the beginning of the year/semester as we have said, but it continues right up to the moment you sit down at that desk in the examination hall. Make sure you are there on time at the right place and on the right date and that you have all the items necessary to do an examination.

Apart from these general and apparently obvious points we feel it necessary to emphasise the following matters:

(a)   Do not just read the examination paper rubric, but also read carefully what any question asks you, for example, does it say 'Discuss' or 'Advise X'. The difference may be crucial. Read the whole of the paper and identify which questions you can and/or wish to answer. Assuming you have not drawn a complete blank, you should seek to identify the legal issues in the problem questions. In essay-type questions you need to devise quickly and briefly a structure for your answer.

(b)   Allocate your time evenly between questions. Some students find it useful to write down finishing and starting times for questions. This problem of making sure you answer or attempt to answer the required number of questions is so often the downfall of many students. It surely is obvious that it is easier to collect more marks on a fresh question than it is to continue writing on a previous topic. The law of diminishing returns has something to do with it. A student who writes too much on a question at the expense of others clearly has not mastered the technique of the examination game.

(c)   Concise, accurate answers are preferable. You should only elaborate on facts of cases where the question demands it, i.e., where the facts of a problem may differ from the facts of a case and you are being asked to decide whether the distinction is material. Regurgitation of all you know on a topic is a common phenomenon and one to be avoided. It shows a lack of discrimination on your part.

(d) This follows on from (c). You should try to answer the question set, not the one you would have liked the examiner to set. You must adapt the material you have revised to suit the demands and requirements of the question being asked. Too often students ignore this advice — they see examinations as being merely a question of showing knowledge to an examiner rather than showing how to use that knowledge to best effect.

(e) Students are often reluctant to evaluate and put forward their own viewpoint on a particular issue. Provided you have arguments to justify your position, you should state your view if the question calls for it. Examiners are looking for signs that students have given some thought to the material and are attempting evaluation. Often questions dictate that a student attempts a critical analysis. For example, the question may say, 'To what extent is it true to say that the duty of care in negligence is really a question of policy?' A student who merely plunges into the appropriate case law without attempting to assess the accuracy of the statement is not really answering the question. The material relating to this question must be geared towards answering it. You could say that policy has no part to play; alternatively, it could be said that policy is the only criterion when deciding whether a negligent defendant owes a duty to an injured plaintiff. The third possibility is that policy is one of the factors, and only one, when a court decides the issue of whether a duty arises in particular circumstances. You should come off the fence and say which of these alternatives you prefer.

In conclusion, we would remind you that the examiner is looking for a legible, well-balanced script which reflects a good assimilation of knowledge combined with an attempt to apply that knowledge in an effort to answer the question set. In the following chapters we will be exploring difficulties with particular substantive topics in the law of torts, but the general points we have discussed so far should not be forgotten.

EXAMINATION TECHNIQUE AND LEGAL PROBLEMS

Whilst the points made above should be sufficient to enable students to cope with essay questions, legal problems and the technique necessary to deal effectively with them deserve more detailed attention. Legal problems are extremely popular with examiners as a means of testing the student's knowledge and understanding. Often by virtue of the number of such questions in an examination paper a student will be compelled to deal with at least one and probably more. In our experience this type of question does appear to cause students more difficulty than essay-type questions. We are of the opinion that a good deal of student underperformance in this connection is due to a lack of the required technique which is, of necessity, more sophisticated than that which is required to respond to essay questions.

We have taken the view that students would probably find it helpful if, in addition to giving guidance as to the technique which they need to acquire, we also gave some insight into the techniques employed by the examiner when constructing problem questions. First, a few words of reassurance. We have already pointed out that examiners are not in the business of trying to fail students. When creating problem questions the examiner will try to ensure that they are balanced and fair and allow a student capable of achieving a pass to do so. By the same token problems must not be pedestrian, so as to prevent the better student from doing justice to himself. There is no golden rule that problem questions suit the better student. Good technique is essential to all students and all are capable of mastering the requisite technique.

The Examiner's Approach

When constructing legal problems the examiner has first to decide what issues he wishes to raise for discussion and secondly how he will do so. The chosen facts must enable the student to identify those issues at least in general terms. Such questions will usually raise a number of issues. These may be confined within the area of one particular tort or they may cross the boundaries between torts and the facts have to be chosen accordingly.

This matter of limitation and identification of issues may also be to some extent dealt with in the rubric to a question. An obvious example of this would be, 'Discuss the possible liability of D in the tort of negligence'. By such an instruction the examiner is ruling out the need to discuss the possible liability of D under any other tort. On the other hand the rubric might simply invite you to 'Discuss' the problem. In such a case you must pay extra special attention to the facts to see, for example, whether they raise the possibility that D might be liable under different torts.

But beware, the guidance to students will almost never be solely confined to the rubric. It is important that students are able to appreciate the legal significance of facts and the examiner will use the facts of questions both to provide guidance and to test that ability. For the same reasons, he may use what is known as the 'omitted fact' technique, i.e., the examiner deliberately omits a legally material fact. Examiners find this a useful ploy for other reasons. Assuming the student spots the omission, he is then forced to speculate, to argue an issue in different ways. Suppose, for example, an examiner wished to raise vicarious liability as a major issue in a problem and wanted students to discuss the principles and cases with regard to both employees and independent contractors. He might in the rubric instruct you to consider, for example, 'the possible liability of D1 and D2'. Then in the problem itself he might portray D2 as being employed by D1 in circumstances in which D2 might be either an employee or an independent contractor, but deliberately omitting to state in which capacity D2 was employed.

An examiner will frequently build in 'prompts' and clues drawing students towards specific issues and even particular cases. Whilst doing so he will avoid using facts which are identical to those in any decided case, for he will be seeking to ensure that students argue through the use of principle and analogy. Gauging the appropriate strength of the 'prompt' can be a difficult exercise, some may be more subtle than others to allow for the varying abilities of students.

Constructing 'good' problems is something of an art. Examiners differ substantially in style and approach. We believe it is enormously helpful for students to become familiar with the style of their particular examiners. In this connection students should obtain and study carefully copies of past examination papers. The problem questions found on seminar sheets are often past examination questions. Where this is so it affords an invaluable opportunity to develop a satisfactory technique long before the dreaded examinations time. We cannot over emphasise the importance of application and practice not only at revision time but throughout the semester or year. Merely reading the advice which follows will assist you very little, the techniques have to be applied.

The Student's Technique

The approach to problem questions has two quite distinct aspects. First, a student must identify as many of the detailed issues as possible and secondly, he has to deal with those issues in a manner which will impress the examiner.

Identification of issues

As we have indicated above guidance as to the identification and limitation of the issues involved may well be contained both in the rubric and the facts of the problem. Read the rubric carefully and note precisely what it requires of you. Now for the facts. Think of the problem question as a carefully constructed crossword puzzle. This is in many respects an accurate analogy. Clues are provided, but you need to think in a particular way. Above all you need concentration, a receptive state of mind and experience gained through practice. There are, we believe, certain techniques which can assist significantly not only in identifying issues but also in promoting a more structured answer.

First, we would draw attention to the usefulness of definitions. Earlier in this chapter in the part on revision we gave warning of that usefulness in this context. When the facts of a problem are searched against a definition which contains, for example, the basic elements of a particular tort, it is far more likely that the right interconnections will be made and the legal issues identified. An important and integral part of this whole process is the making of a rough plan in note form. The plan should begin with the definition itself. As you search through a problem identifying issues, the detailed points and relevant case law which spring to mind should be briefly noted. This plan should then be used as the basis for your answer. No doubt as you consider and write the final version of your answer further relevant material will be recalled which you will wish to incorporate therein.

These rough plans are not only helpful in terms of the contents of your answers but may also assist enormously in achieving a sensible structure and balance. Difficulties in structuring an answer may well be exacerbated, for example, by the presence in the problem of two or more potential plaintiffs and/or defendants. Preparatory work along the lines indicated will, in so far as it reveals the number of relevant issues involved, allow the student to balance the depth of treatment given to individual issues with the need to say something meaningful about all of them.

Anxiety experienced in examinations often leads students to neglect this preparatory work. The failure to identify important issues, lack of structure, unbalanced treatment of the recognised issues, are the hallmarks of an ill-prepared answer. The message is loud and clear. Time spent in preparing answers using the above-mentioned techniques, whether or not under examination conditions, is an invaluable investment.

Dealing with the issues
In order to avoid underperformance students must develop the skills which are necessary to communicate effectively via the medium of the legal problem: a medium which requires the application of knowledge to hypothetical situations. Effective communication involves considerations of both content and style. Students must ensure at all times that the material deployed in their answers is relevant. The sheer bulk of relevant material and the severe constraints upon time in examinations pose problems of selection and treatment. Students often leave examination rooms expressing their disappointment that they 'knew all the stuff' but 'didn't have time to get it all down'. This may well reflect inadequate examination technique. The advice which follows is given to enable students to avoid such disappointment which all too frequently results from poor examination technique. We repeat an earlier observation that a number of points made below appear to be so obvious as not to require stating. That unfortunately has not been our experience.

(a) A basic error which is perhaps more common amongst mature students on the first year of either a full-time or part-time course, is that they suggest solutions to problems in commonsense terms rather than by way of legal principles and decided cases. Often such answers have very little of the law in them and will gain very few marks indeed.

(b)   When answering examination questions, whether essays or problems, the unselective regurgitation of notes, even if verbatim, is hardly a satisfactory approach. Students must demonstrate their understanding through the selective application of principles and cases to move towards a solution to a problem.

(c)   Be prepared to adopt a standpoint and argue. An examiner not only hopes for argument but expects it. Often he will have chosen to raise an issue on which the authorities support the possibility of tenable alternative views. The absence of authority supporting a particular viewpoint should not of itself be regarded as a bar to argument. It is not of any great significance that the examiner and yourself reach different conclusions, unless that demonstrates misunderstanding on your part.

Relevance
On the general point of ensuring that the material deployed is relevant the following should be borne in mind:

(a)   When dealing with a problem question do not write a long-winded, general and/or historical introduction to the relevant area of law. You may state briefly how you intend approaching the problem and then embark immediately upon providing answers on the specific points which you have identified. The following illustration from our own past experience should hopefully make the point.

A problem was set which was concerned with the tort of negligence in which one potential defendant, an 84-year-old man, collapsed whilst driving his car on the highway. This resulted in a further sequence of events with which we need not concern ourselves here. In lectures the lecturer concerned had outlined the historical development of negligence as a nominate tort in its own right. This was but a prelude to the more detailed examination of the modern position wherein the application of the tort to a wide range of situations, including road traffic, was conveyed.

A number of students who attempted that question actually reproduced information as to the historical development of negligence, in some cases extending to almost a full page of writing. This is a clear example of blind, unthinking regurgitation, and an appalling waste of the students' time and effort. An introduction along the following lines would have been infinitely preferable.

It is well established in principle and case law that the drivers of motor vehicles upon the highway owe a duty of reasonable care. The immediate questions are: To whom do they owe such duty and, what is the standard of care which is required of them?

(b)   One matter with which many students experience difficulty is how much of the facts of cases they should incorporate into their answers. Evidence of that difficulty is to be found in the extreme positions adopted in numerous examination scripts. Some students appear to be totally averse to ever stating facts, whilst others insist upon devoting half a page to the facts of a simple case. In the former situation the student's level of knowledge may not be effectively communicated to the examiner, whilst a student indulging in the latter practice may to some extent be wasting valuable time.

As a working rule you should state only those facts which are necessary in support of the particular point of law which you assert. With regard to 'landmark' cases such as *Donoghue* v *Stevenson*, you may safely assume that the examiner is aware of the facts. Do not insist upon informing him in graphic detail of the alleged presence of the decomposed snail in a bottle of ginger-ale. On the other hand it may be appropriate to refer specifically to the facts of cases, even to those of the 'landmark' decisions. The following illustration will hopefully demonstrate that it is quite within the grasp of most if not all students to incorporate authorities into an answer in a way which clearly conveys the relevance of a decision to the point of law in question, whilst at the same time avoiding the need to state the detailed facts of that decision.

Suppose you were dealing with a problem concerning the extent to which pure economic loss was recoverable in the tort of negligence. You would no doubt wish to point out that the duty of care in this context is not confined to situations in which the actual identity of the plaintiff is known to the defendant, but extends to other situations where the plaintiff is readily identifiable. This could be supported in the following terms:

Such a position was clearly anticipated by the House of Lords on the facts, in the seminal decision in *Hedley Byrne* v *Heller*.

As examiners we would accept that statement as an adequate demonstration that a student understood the material facts of *Hedley Byrne* without him having spelled them out in a more detailed statement occupying a further three or four lines.

A good answer to a question will obviously demonstrate a thorough knowledge of case law on a particular topic. Such an answer will not only explain the relevance of certain decisions, but will also explain why other decisions are not regarded as relevant. We have already warned that the facts of the problem may well have been carefully chosen in order to provoke and facilitate this kind of discussion. In giving such an answer a student may well be involved in handling a significant number of authorities. Many students simply lack the necessary technique to do so. We suspect that some students appreciate that certain cases which appear to be relevant on the facts of the problem may be properly distinguished. But they refuse to become involved in saying so simply through pressure of time. We know that other students try to deal with this matter by stating, for example, 'The decision in *Smith* v *Jones* is distinguishable', but fail to give any explanation as to why this may be so. At the other extreme, in distinguishing a single case, some students allow themselves to be drawn into making a far more detailed statement of facts than is necessary and find they have insufficient time to deal adequately with other issues they have identified. These difficulties may be avoided by adopting a style similar to that above which should enable you to say a good deal in relatively few words. Furthermore, your script is likely to be far more readable, a point which may count substantially in your favour in the tired eyes of the examiner.

We would describe such a style as 'functional'. It should help you cope more adequately with the demands of examinations. However, this impressionism should not be carried too far. Try to ensure that your style overtly demonstrates your understanding of the authorities. On the other hand you should make every effort to avoid writing an answer the text of which is interspersed with, indeed interrupted by, 'block' statements of detailed factual information. The names of cases can and should be memorised. They facilitate the employment of the style advocated above. Valuable time might otherwise be wasted by having to identify cases by stating their facts. However, as a final resort you may do so and you should recognise that the level of the decision and its date is of greater significance than the name of the case. From a presentational point of view it is customary wisdom to advise students to physically underline the names of cases incorporated in their answers so as to emphasise their presence and thus impress the examiner.

(c) We believe it is important that students should have a clear understanding of when and to what degree it may be appropriate to speculate on facts other than those set out in a problem, especially in view of the possible use by an examiner of the 'omitted fact' technique. To this end the following advice should not only be borne in mind but put into practice:

(i)   Do not speculate on facts contrary to those actually stated in a problem unless the examiner specifically asks you to do so.

(ii)   Be prepared to recognise that legally relevant facts may be implicitly stated in a problem and deal with them accordingly.

(iii) Approach problem questions on the assumption that certain legally relevant facts may well have been omitted. Obviously your ability to identify as relevant, facts which are omitted, comes from your detailed knowledge of case law. If you feel you have identified a legally relevant fact which is not stated in the problem you should hypothesise as to what the legal solution may be alternatively taking into account the presence of the fact and its absence.

In the following problem we have sought to illustrate further these three basic points:

> D, the manager of a public house invited several of his friends, including Paul, to an 'after hours' drinking party in private rooms above the public bar. Paul left the party alone at 2 a.m. He fell down the stairs leading from the private rooms and was killed.
> Discuss.

This briefly stated problem calls upon students to engage in a substantial amount of speculation as to facts and the detailed issues which might be involved. Considerable guidance in that respect is given since the facts stated do, to some extent, resemble those of two reasonably well-known cases on the question of occupiers' liability.

(a)   First, by stating that 'D is the manager of a public house', we tried to imply that some other person (O) might be the owner thus creating the possiblity that both D and O could be occupiers for the purposes of the Occupiers' Liability Act 1957. We would expect students to recognise this possibility and discuss the question of their respective duties which they might owe to P in the light of cases such as *Wheat v E. Lacon & Co. Ltd* [1966] AC 552 and *Stone v Taffe* [1974] 1 WLR 1575.

(b)   Though no mention is made in the problem of any restriction placed by O upon the authority of D to allow parties of this kind, such a restriction and its effectiveness was at issue in *Stone v Taffe* and other decisions. This should lead students on to discuss the further possibility that as against O, P might be either (1) a lawful visitor to whom O owed a duty of reasonable care under the Occupiers' Liability Act 1957 or (2) a trespasser to whom O owed only the lower standard of care by virtue of the Occupiers' Liability Act 1984.

(c)   Further speculation is required on the student's part with regard to the possible cause of the accident. We would expect this to include an explanation of the relevance and degree of control over such cause as might have been exercised by D and O respectively, as to which see *Wheat v E. Lacon & Co. Ltd* [1966] AC 552.

Students would also be expected to consider the possibility that Paul might have been under the influence of drink when he fell and to explain the relevance of such a fact in the context of defences of which both D and O might avail themselves. What we would hope not to see is speculation that

Paul might have been pushed by another guest. We believe we gave reasonable warning against this in the problem by stating that 'Paul left the party alone'.

SUMMARY

In chapters 1 and 2 we have drawn attention to, and advised how to avoid, what we perceive as the major failures in study methods and examination and assessment technique. We have sought to illustrate that advice at various points. In doing so we inevitably became involved with the substance of the law of torts. These illustrations should become more meaningful as you progress through the course and acquire knowledge of relevant areas of law. In subsequent chapters we take this illustrative approach much further. Our purpose is to enable students to gain progressively the experience and practice which are important to the development of a satisfactory examination technique. We also hope that the chapter will enable students to perform better in the coursework, if assessed, throughout the semester or academic year.

3 TRESPASS TO THE PERSON

INTRODUCTION

In this chapter we shall concern ourselves only with the torts of assault and battery, to the exclusion of false imprisonment which is traditionally taught in the civil liberties context in a constitutional law syllabus. The proportion of victims of assault and battery who receive compensation via the civil process is probably quite small in relation to the number of assaults and batteries committed on a daily basis. The reasons for this are pragmatic: the poverty of many potential defendants is an effective practical bar to a civil action. Indeed, the Criminal Injuries Compensation Scheme is a more realistic source of compensation in these circumstances, for it should be noted that assault and battery are not only civil wrongs but may also amount to criminal offences. The scheme has now been placed on a statutory footing by the Criminal Justice Act 1988 (though this change has yet to be implemented), and provides compensation broadly in line with the common law in most circumstances but the government has proposed changes to this. One exception appears to be victims of rape. The amounts awarded under the scheme appear to be significantly lower than those awarded under the common law (see *Meah* v *McCreamer (No. 1)* [1985] 1 All ER 367). These torts, nonetheless, do have practical significance. This may well lie in their connection with other available remedies, for example, self-defence, and in certain circumstances injunctions. The recent majority decision of the Court of Appeal in *Khorasandjian* v *Bush* [1993] 3 WLR 476, is particularly interesting in this latter respect (see below).

Quite apart from practical considerations, there are, in addition, sound academic reasons why these two torts might be included in any teaching syllabus. Assault and battery are useful topics by means of which students can be introduced to legal concepts which are regarded as slightly easier to grasp. Furthermore, trespass to the person generally gives a valuable insight into the historical development of the law of torts, in particular the more modern tort of negligence.

SUBSTANTIVE DIFFICULTIES

Assault and battery are each independent torts in their own right. This distinction in the civil law of torts is something with which students initially experience some difficulty. We suspect that this may stem from the way in which the term 'assault and battery' is used to denote a single offence in the criminal law. Such offences are commonly reported in newspapers simply as assault, which only adds to the confusion. The tortious meanings of assault and battery are discussed fully in the 'Commentary' section of this chapter. Suffice it to say at this stage that an assault is committed simply by causing someone to apprehend unlawful contact with his person, whereas battery is the intentional unlawful contact itself. Thus, for example, an actionable assault would be clearly committed if, without lawful excuse, the defendant swung a punch at the plaintiff, but missed.

Despite the fact that they are separate torts a number of issues which cause difficulty to students are common to both.

Directness of harm
One major limitation of the 'great' writ of trespass is that an action will lie only with regard to certain types of harm which are *directly inflicted* by the defendant upon the plaintiff. Although there has been some widening of the notion of 'directness' (see *Scott v Shepherd* (1773) 2 Bl R 892), it remains, at least in English law, a significant restriction upon the scope of both assault and battery.

This classification of actions according to a particular causal concept is incompatible with the modern trend which categorises claims according to the nature of the defendant's conduct, i.e., was it intentional or unintentional (see Lord Denning MR in *Letang v Cooper* [1965] 1 QB 232 at p. 349). Whether or not an action will now lie in trespass where the harm is inflicted unintentionally but negligently is considered below. Even where the harm is intentionally inflicted two other quite distinct points need to be made.

Actionable without proof of damage
Students frequently misunderstand the nature of the interference which will give rise to an action in assault and battery. Both torts are actionable *per se*

and this means, in simple terms, that the plaintiff is entitled to damages even though the interference has caused him no physical injury, damage to his property or financial loss. This, of course, is not so where an action is brought 'on the case' as in *Wilkinson* v *Downton* [1897] 2 QB 57, or in the tort of negligence. Both required proof of actual damage. A useful illustration of trespass being actionable *per se* might be the non-violent unlawful taking of fingerprints, where, if substantial damages are awarded, this is primarily compensation for an interference with one's freedom.

What kind of harm is actionable in trespass?
This is a relatively straightforward question in battery — the 'harm' is the actual unlawful physical contact. There are, however, many instances of what we shall loosely term antisocial behaviour which may give rise to a variety of unpleasant, emotional experiences. An action in assault will lie where the defendant's behaviour causes the plaintiff to reasonably apprehend an immediate contact with his person. It will be actionable irrespective of whether fear is experienced by the victim. However, other emotional experiences, unpleasant though they may be, may be actionable in some other tort, for example, defamation, where insulting words are used.

There is some confusion in the case law which amounts to a failure to recognise that the question of 'reasonable apprehension of the plaintiff' should be approached from the perspective of the reasonable man in the shoes of the plaintiff, and not necessarily from the standpoint of the defendant's lack of ability or intent to batter the plaintiff. This particular issue has arisen in a number of cases concerning unloaded guns.

In many cases of assault the threatening behaviour may well encompass not just physical acts but also words. More often than not the words used will confirm a reasonable apprehension of a battery. Occasionally, the words used may negate any such apprehension. An examiner may wish to test a student's appreciation of the relevance of words in the context of assault. This leads us to an issue of principle, namely, whether an assault may be committed by words. There are differing opinions on this issue both in the case law and amongst academics.

It has to be recognised that assault as a tort (and indeed battery) has its limitations and falls far short of any universal principle providing redress for every conceivable type of harm which might be intentionally inflicted. For example, it is quite possible to cause harm through words or conduct, which is not actionable as an assault, but which may fall within the scope of some other nominate or innominate tort such as *Wilkinson* v *Downton* [1897] 2 QB 57. The intentional harassment of another person such as arose in the recent case of *Khorasandjian* v *Bush* [1993] 3 WLR 476, is an excellent example of this. In that case the Court of Appeal, by a majority of 2–1, upheld the grant of an injunction. In so doing the court appears not only to have extended the principle in *Wilkinson* v *Downton*, but has also removed the need for a plaintiff to have an interest in land in order to have an action in private nuisance (see chapter 10). This is one example where a question might cross the traditional boundaries of individual torts and accordingly prove popular with examiners.

The state of mind of the defendant

Assuming that the plaintiff is directly affected by the defendant's voluntary act, four important questions arise as to the state of mind of the defendant required in the tort of trespass to the person.

(a) Where the conduct is said to be 'intentional', what is it that the defendant must intend? Students are often unclear on this matter. Where the plaintiff alleges an intentional battery, what he must show is that the defendant *intended the contact*; it is not necessary to show that the defendant intended the harmful consequence (if any) which flowed from the contact. See *Williams* v *Humphrey* (1975) *The Times*, 20 February; *Wilson* v *Pringle* [1986] 3 WLR 1.

(b) What precisely amounts to 'intentional' contact in this context? Contact which the defendant desired will certainly be intentional, as will contacts which are undesired but which are on the facts substantially certain to result from the defendant's conduct. Whilst there appear to be no modern cases covering precisely this latter point on battery, the decision in *Wilkinson* v *Downton* (1897) (above) arguably supports that view. Students will recognise this case as one in which a practical joke went wrong. Of the untrue statement made by the defendant practical joker (that the plaintiff's husband had been injured in an accident), Wright said: 'it is difficult to imagine that such a statement, made suddenly and with apparent seriousness, could fail to produce grave effects ... and therefore an intention to produce such an effect must be imputed.'

Recklessness may also be sufficient to found a civil action in assault or battery, though again there is a dearth of modern authority directly in point (i.e., a reckless act may be treated as an intentional act). Thus, even though contact may not be desired nor substantially certain to result from the defendant's conduct, if the defendant knows that contact may well result from his actions and carries on, taking the risk, not caring whether the contact occurs, he may be liable in battery. The absence in civil law of a doctrine of transferred malice could make the issue of recklessness important in an action in trespass. Beware, therefore, of examination questions in which, for example, blows or objects thrown at one person strike another.

(c) Can a person be liable in battery where an unintentional but negligent act causes direct contact with another person? Though there is some authority for the proposition that trespass can only be committed by intentional conduct (including recklessness), it cannot be regarded as finally settled. (See Street, *On Torts*, 9th edn, p. 17). According to Lord Denning MR (with whom Danckwerts LJ agreed) in *Letang* v *Cooper* [1965] 1 QB 232 at p. 240, where the conduct complained of is unintentional though arguably negligent, the plaintiff's case must be pleaded in the tort of negligence. That view recently received further support from dicta in the Court of Appeal in *Wilson* v *Pringle* [1986] 2 WLR 1 (per Croom-Johnson LJ at p. 8).

Even if an action can be maintained in trespass for unintentional but negligent conduct, it may be that most, if not all the advantages of such an action over an action in negligence have been removed. Again the authorities through which this apparent rationalisation of negligence/trespass has been achieved are not 'fireproof'. Examiners may well seek to test the student's knowledge and understanding of this issue. We would advise students to consider carefully what possible differences exist between an action for negligent trespass and an action in the tort of negligence, if they are indeed alternative to each other.

(d)   Must the intention of the defendant be in some way 'hostile'? As a matter of general principle battery protects not only from injury but also against other forms of physical molestation, subject to the requirement of the absence of consent on the part of the plaintiff. Just as the unwanted blow is a battery so also is an unwanted kiss. However, in *Wilson* v *Pringle* (above) the Court of Appeal held that unless it is self-evident from the act itself the plaintiff must plead facts which show the contact to be hostile. The difficulty with this case is that it is by no means clear what is meant by 'hostility', since both the cases used by the court to illustrate what turns a friendly touching (which is not actionable) into an unfriendly one (which is) are cases in which there was an absence of consent to the touching, which was therefore unlawful. If hostility is an additional requirement to that of the absence of consent, it would be interesting to know whether or not the short-sighted surgeon who mistakenly performs a vasectomy instead of a tonsillectomy would be guilty of a battery.

In two recent cases concerning the lawfulness of the sterilisation of mentally handicapped persons, hostility as an additional requirement to the absence of consent has been rejected. See *T* v *T* [1988] 2 WLR 189 and *F* v *West Berkshire Health Authority* [1989] 2 All ER 545, HL. In the latter case, Lord Goff expressed the view, at p. 564, that:

A prank which gets out of hand, an overfriendly slap on the back, surgical treatment by a surgeon who mistakenly thinks that the patient has consented to it, all these things may transcend the bounds of lawfulness without being characterised as hostile.

We do not doubt that your examiners are capable of raising other interesting questions on this issue. Further and equally uncomfortable thoughts on mishaps in the course of medical treatment are expressed below in connection with the defence of consent.

Defences

There are a number of defences which may be wholly or partially successful. These include provocation, self-defence and consent. Whilst there are some similarities and possible overlap between these defences they are technically distinct, and may be pleaded in the alternative in a case, depending upon the facts. The major issue, as far as provocation is concerned, is whether it affords a full or only a partial defence. Can insulting words in law ever justify a battery? As to self-defence, the difficulty here is whether the nature of the response is 'reasonable' as is required in law. In principle this right extends to defending other persons and indeed property. Is it permissible to use the same degree of force in both cases?

One defence which deserves special mention is that of consent. This is a defence of general application in the law of torts although it appears in different guises with different labels, for example, *volenti non fit injuria* in negligence, licence in respect of trespass to land. In the context of an alleged assault and battery, consent may well be either express or implied. Particular problems have arisen recently in respect of sporting activities and medical treatment. The kind of questions that have arisen in recent cases have been concerned with such matters as the extent of implied consent to injuries sustained as a result of foul play in soccer and rugby in particular. Is every injury caused by conduct outside the rules of the relevant game actionable? There have also been some interesting and controversial cases, for example, on the forced feeding of prisoners on hunger strike. The question which requires consideration is not whether the prisoner consents, which he may well not do, but whether there are other policy grounds upon which such feeding can be justified.

The issue of consent has proved somewhat troublesome in the context of medical treatment. In a number of recent cases members of the judiciary have expressed their disapproval of the pleading of an action in battery (as an alternative to negligence), in circumstances where doctors have allegedly failed to disclose sufficiently the risks inherent in medical treatment. (See, for example, Lord Scarman in *Sidaway* v *Bethlem Royal Hospital Governors* [1985] 1 All ER 643 at p. 650, who thought such pleading 'deplorable'). The sensitivity of the judiciary to the conclusion that a failure to advise adequately as to inherent risks (thus negating consent) means that the doctor has battered the patient, has led to strong views being expressed that such cases are actionable only in the tort of negligence. In *Sidaway's* case the House of Lords substantially confirmed that the principle laid down in *Bolam* v *Friern Hospital Management Committee* [1957] 1 WLR 582 (discussed in chapter 4 below) is applicable not only to negligent diagnosis and treatment cases, but also to the extent to which inherent risks should be disclosed to patients. This, however, falls far short of the doctrine of 'informed consent' as developed in the USA and Canada. Despite the judicial disapproval noted above, certain types of 'medical mishaps' will continue to be actionable in battery, where for example the 'wrong' operation is performed on the 'right' patient or where the 'right' operation is performed on the 'wrong' patient, there is no consent as to the nature of the treatment itself. Students should not be surprised to find questions on this area continuing to appear on examination papers. The issue is a controversial one and it cuts across the boundaries of two torts, trespass and negligence. A student would probably be better able to impress the examiner if he were to read and to digest the major points in the article by Feng (1987) *The Journal of Legal Studies,* p. 149.

Students might also give some thought to the potential advantages (if any) of suing in trespass as opposed to negligence (where possible). That question is unfortunately not addressed by the learned author of the above-mentioned article.

In addition to the above-mentioned defences, in certain circumstances the courts are prepared to invoke another principle founded on policy, namely, *ex turpi causa non oritur actio,* for example, where either one or both parties to an action are involved in some criminal activity. The effect this may have is to deprive one or both of the parties of redress in a civil action. The precise scope of this principle is not altogether clear, which makes it an attractive topic to an examiner.

ILLUSTRATIVE PROBLEM

Roughneck and his girlfriend, Gloria, after an afternoon drinking session, are at the station waiting for a train home during the rush hour. James, one of the many commuters pouring on to the platform, pushes past Roughneck catching him with his briefcase. There follows an angry exchange of words during which James calls Roughneck an 'ill-bred lout' and Gloria 'a drunken slut'. Gloria lashes out at James but misses him. Her further attempts to strike James are restrained by bystanders. In the meantime, Roughneck advances on James with fists clenched. The latter raises his umbrella and prods Roughneck gently in the stomach. Roughneck responds by giving James a violent push knocking him into an old lady, Lucy, standing close to the platform edge. Lucy falls and is struck and injured by an oncoming train. Discuss.

COMMENTARY

Applying the advice in the previous chapter we would suggest consideration be given to the following points concerning both examination technique and substantive issues.

Structure of an Answer

In your rough plan you should have included definitions of assault and battery, for example, those in Winfield and Jolowicz (13th ed.). Assault is there defined as 'an act of the defendant which causes to the plaintiff reasonable apprehension of the infliction of a battery on him by the defendant'. Battery is defined as 'the intentional and direct application of force to another person'. The facts of the problem should be searched against those definitions and a note of the issues raised; in so doing you should scrutinise very carefully the wording of the problem and be watchful for 'prompts'. In view of the number of potential plaintiffs and defendants, the answer will need to be structured to avoid repetition and confusion. The structure which we have adopted is as follows:

(a)   James (J) against Roughneck (R).
(b)   J against Gloria (G).
(c)   Lucy (L) against J and R.

Within this structure we have elected to deal with the issues in a chronological order. We consider this approach particularly appropriate in this context, because, for example, the question as to whether J has committed a battery or is exercising his legitimate right to self-defence depends to some extent on whether R's earlier action constitutes an assault.

J v R

The first issue that arises is whether J's direct contact with R amounts to a battery. There are two possible ways of viewing this incident. It could be argued that there is technically a battery subject to the defence of implied consent (see, e.g., *Coward* v *Baddeley* (1859) 4 H & N 478). Alternatively, it could be and has been said that there is no battery at all. In *Cole* v *Turner* (1704) 6 Mod 149 Holt CJ took the view that 'if two or more meet in a narrow passage, and without any violence or design of harm, the one touches the other gently, it will be no battery'. Whichever of these two approaches is adopted the policy of excluding trivial though frequent incidents from the ambit of trespass is clear. A further possible argument on this point is whether the contact was intentional. This is specifically referred to by Holt CJ when, to use his phrase, the contact is without 'design of harm' and will be discussed in more depth below.

The next point arises in connection with the phrase 'an angry exchange of words'. In view of the vague nature of that phrase, it is probably only worth while making comments of a most general nature, for example, that such an exchange might be relevant to the defence of provocation. In the light of J's reference to R as 'an ill-bred lout', it is far better to devote your efforts to a discussion of that with regard to provocation.

The next issue is R's advance on J with clenched fists. Prima facie, this is an assault since his behaviour could easily lead a reasonable man to apprehend immediate contact with his person. The facts on this point have been chosen deliberately to draw the student's attention to the decision in *Read v Coker* (1853) 13 CB 850. As we have already indicated it is open to R to raise the defence of provocation. There appears to be a dearth of authority as to whether provocation may be either a full or even a partial defence to the tort of assault. If the principles with regard to battery were adopted, then provocation may be relied upon as a partial defence, which much resembles the defence of contributory negligence. Indeed, according to the dictum of Lord Denning MR in *Murphy v Culhane* [1977] QB 94 at p. 96 the defence of contributory negligence may apply to the tort of battery. If this were so then the defence of provocation would, in certain circumstances, be superfluous. As a partial defence only, provocation may be taken into account only to the extent of reducing the exemplary or aggravated damages aspect of an award (see *Lane v Holloway* [1968] 1 QB 379). If, as suggested by Lord Denning, the Law Reform (Contributory Negligence) Act 1945 were to apply, there would be scope for greater reduction in the damages otherwise awarded. In an unreported case the Court of Appeal has now accepted (obiter) that the defence of contributory negligence may be raised in an action alleging an intentional battery; see *Barnes v Nayer* (1986) *The Times*, 19 December.

The next matter to consider is the action of J in prodding R gently in the stomach with the umbrella. Since the defence of provocation is unlikely to negate the assault, then J may well argue that this is an act of self-defence, in the event that R claims it to be a battery. The principle governing this defence is that of reasonable force in the circumstances, see, for example, *Cockroft v Smith* (1705) 2 Salk 642. It would seem that J's action does not exceed the bounds of reasonable force and is, therefore, a lawful excuse. A possible alternative argument which might be put on behalf of J which should be dealt with in the light of the recent decision of the Court of Appeal in *Wilson v Pringle* (above), is that the contact did not constitute a battery because although the contact was intentional it was not hostile. If an answer dealing with this point is to impress an examiner it would need to show some understanding of the difficulty surrounding this issue, to which we referred earlier in this chapter.

It seems from the above discussion that R might well be found liable in both assault and battery to J. As a last resort, R might seek to rely on the maxim *ex turpi causa non oritur actio*. That plea was rejected in *Lane v Holloway* [1968] 1 QB 379 on the grounds that the blow was out of all proportion to the provocation and the blow sustained by the defendant. The parties were not, therefore, regarded as being in pari delicto. It would appear that the person perceived to be the most blameworthy may not be allowed to sue in respect of his own injury (see *Murphy* v *Culhane* [1977] QB 94), or to set up the maxim to defeat the claim by the other party. On the facts of this problem, the plea would probably fail.

J v G

G's attempt to strike J could clearly constitute an assault, assuming J saw the attempt, even though there was no contact. In addition, the further attempts to strike J may also constitute assault, if on the facts this would cause a reasonable person to apprehend bodily contact. There is a clear prompt here towards the decision of *Stephens* v *Myers* (1830) 4 C & P 349. The words uttered by J may well be relevant in two senses. First, they might in theory give rise to an action in defamation, whilst not giving rise to an actionable assault in themselves. Secondly, G might argue that the words amounted to provocation, as to which see the discussion above.

L v J and R

Whilst the action by L against J and R may be against them as joint tortfeasors, the arguments raised by each of the defendants against their individual liability in trespass may be quite different. In order to avoid confusion it makes sense, therefore, to deal with the defendants separately.

L v J

There has clearly been bodily contact, but since this resulted from an 'involuntary act' by J, this would not constitute a battery. In addition, it would seem difficult to argue that J caused the contact either intentionally or recklessly. However, a possible action in negligence might lie on the grounds that L's injury was a foreseeable result of the fracas in which J was involved.

L v R

The first difficulty in establishing battery against R is that R appears to lack the requisite state of mind, namely intention. Furthermore, English tort law does not recognise any doctrine of transferred intention. It might, however, be argued that he was reckless as against L. If that argument succeeded it would be sufficient to establish liability subject to what is said below. The further question arises as to whether the contact between L and J was directly caused by R. The case of *Scott* v *Shepherd* (1773) 2 Bl R 892 might be used to support the argument that this was sufficiently direct.

In the event that the above two requirements are not satisfied, then an alternative action might be framed in negligence. Indeed, there are dicta by

Lord Denning MR in *Letang* v *Cooper* [1965] 1 QB 232 at pp. 239-40 and by Croom-Johnson LJ in *Wilson* v *Pringle* [1986] 3 WLR 1 to the effect that where the contact is unintentionally but negligently inflicted, whether direct or not, the appropriate cause of action is negligence. In practice at least, these statements have effectively settled the issue. However, the matter cannot be regarded as being finally settled (see Diplock LJ in *Letang* v *Cooper* (at p. 243) and *Williams* v *Humphrey* (1975) *The Times*, 20 February). On the facts it is more than likely that the action would be framed in negligence and that there would be liability under the reasonable foresight principle. Both J and R might well be joint tortfeasors, subject to the possible defence of contributory negligence by L in standing near to the platform edge.

ILLUSTRATIVE QUESTION

Now try this one!

Albert, a 14 year-old boy shouts abuse and uses his hands to make insulting gestures at a group of schoolboys as he rides past them on his bicycle. Fred, one of this group, throws his cap in the direction of Albert. Albert loses his balance, falls into the road and breaks his arm. He suffers further injury when, as he lies there, he is struck by a motor vehicle.

Discuss the possible tortious liability of Fred and the motorist.

SELECTED READING

Bridgeman and Jones, 'Harrassing Conduct and Outrageous Acts: A Cause of Action for Intentionally Inflicted Mental Distress' (1994) 14 LS 180.
Hudson, 'Contributory Negligence as a Defence to Battery' (1984) 4 LS 332.
North, 'Civil and Criminal Proceedings for Assault' (1966) 29 MLR 16.
Feng, 'Failure of Medical Advice: Trespass or Negligence' (1987) 7 LS 149.
Trindade, 'Some Curiosities of Negligent Trespass to the Person: A Comparative Study' (1971) 20 ICLQ 706.
Trindade, 'Intentional Torts: Some Thoughts on Assault and Battery' (1982) 2 OJLS 211.

4 NEGLIGENCE 1

INTRODUCTION

In dealing with the tort of negligence we are not concerned so much with historical development but rather with the tort in its present state. Our priority is to identify those aspects of the tort and certain related matters with which students experience difficulty and which are commonly found in examination questions on the subject.

The practical and academic importance of the tort has increased enormously since the now famous dictum of Lord Atkin in *Donoghue* v *Stevenson* [1932] AC 562, at p. 580. The subsequent development of negligence as a tort in its own right has led to substantial inroads being made into other areas traditionally governed by older-established torts (see, for example, the dictum of Lord Denning MR in *Letang* v *Cooper* [1965] 1 QB 232 at p. 240). Not surprisingly, the tort represents a substantial proportion of most, if not all, syllabuses. Indeed, in some institutions negligence together with other matters such as defences, limitations, and the principles of vicarious liability and assessment of damages, comprises the whole syllabus. In other academic establishments the syllabuses are centred upon the debate concerning the respective merits of the tort of negligence and the state system as alternative means of providing compensation for personal injuries.

We shall not be involved in that debate as such nor have we made the above-mentioned matters such as defences, limitations etc. the subject of separate individual treatment. We recognise that any one of those issues may be the subject of an examination question in its own right, though these would tend to be of the essay type. Alternatively, those issues may be raised as ancillary matters in problem questions on negligence. Given the practical limits of a book of this nature the need for compromise has led us to treat these related matters in the latter context. We have therefore included points which touch upon those matters in the illustrative problems and, where they arise we offer brief, though hopefully helpful, commentary upon them in terms of examination technique.

We have sought to recognise the importance of the tort of negligence as a whole by devoting to it several chapters. In this chapter together with chapters 5 and 6 we follow the traditional analysis of the general principles applicable to the existence of a duty of care, breach of the duty of care, causation and remoteness of damage. It is well recognised that there are certain situations wherein those general principles are not applied at all or are not applied in their full rigour. We consider certain of those areas in separate chapters. In chapter 7 we examine the liability of occupiers and non-occupiers for defective premises. In chapters 8 and 9 we consider in some depth the difficulties of applying the general principles of negligence to certain types of harm, namely, economic loss and psychical injury sustained through shock rather than impact.

THE DUTY OF CARE IN THE TORT OF NEGLIGENCE

The Substantive Difficulties

The theoretical (or 'notional') duty of care
In a conceptual sense negligence is a most difficult tort. 'Much of the trouble has stemmed from conceptualising 'duty', 'breach' and 'remoteness' and the superimposition of needless terminological confusion through the indiscriminate use of technical jargon in different senses' (*Clerk and Lindsell on Torts*, 16th ed., p. 610). The issue of the existence and content of a theoretical duty of care contributes significantly to this conceptual confusion. From an examination point of view the issue of the existence of a duty can realistically only be examined as a whole by way of an essay-type question, though specific aspects of the issue or its application in particular fact situations may well be raised as part of a problem-type question. For these reasons the illustrative question used in this chapter is of the essay type and the matter of specific application is taken up in the later chapters concerning, for example, economic loss and nervous shock.

The difficulty which students experience with regard to the theoretical duty of care lies not so much in identifying the problem but rather in understanding the explanation. Let us begin with a very basic question: Why ask whether there is a duty in law to exercise reasonable care so as to avoid injuring people, damaging their property or causing them financial loss? Students themselves realise that we do not ask similar questions in the context of other torts. The reason for this is that a duty not to assault, batter or defame people, for example, is simply assumed to exist. Why is this not so with regard to the tort of negligence? The explanation concerns the fact that the duty of care in negligence is expressed in extremely wide terms, namely that *whenever* a person can reasonably foresee harm to another he owes a duty to exercise reasonable care to avoid causing that harm. In addition the same formulation is employed to decide certain questions involving the further issues of breach of the duty of care and the remoteness of damage. Furthermore there is theoretically no limit to the type of harm to which the tort of negligence can apply, be it personal injury, damage to property or financial loss. Thus the establishment of a duty of reasonable care opens the gate to an enormous field of potential liability, with the prospect of litigation on a scale which would swamp the legal system as we know it. By comparison (as we have seen) the torts of assault and battery are restricted to certain types of harm which are inflicted directly. There is therefore little prospect of opening the floodgates by accepting that there exists a general duty in law to abstain from assaulting and battering people.

The difficulties arising from the width of the duty principle and its place within the conceptual framework of the tort of negligence as a whole have been demonstrated by the interpretation and application of the now discredited dictum of Lord Wilberforce in *Anns* v *Merton London Borough Council* [1978] AC 728 at pp. 751-2. In essence Lord Wilberforce appeared to state that if the type of harm sustained by the plaintiff was reasonably foreseeable there existed a prima facie duty of care subject to any policy considerations which might justify the exclusion of, or restriction being placed upon, that duty. The scope of the general principle and its application in specific situations is now clearly subject to the control device of 'considerations of policy'. This should not be taken to mean that policy considerations have only recently become relevant, for that is not the case; it is simply that in recent times the courts have been more willing to acknowledge the role of policy in the decision-making process. In the context of the difficulties of the conceptual framework of the tort Lord Denning MR observed:

> The more I think about these cases, the more difficult I find it to put each into its proper pigeon-hole. Sometimes I say: 'There was no duty'. In others I say: 'The damage was too remote'. So much so that I think the time has come to discard those tests which have proved so elusive. It seems to me better to consider the particular relationship in hand, and see whether or not, as a matter of policy, [the] loss should be recoverable (*Spartan Steel & Alloys Ltd* v *Martin & Co. (Contractors) Ltd* [1973] QB 27, at p. 37.)

In the earlier editions of this book we indicated that the 'two-stage' approach advocated by Lord Wilberforce in *Anns* was then the subject of some criticism 'on the grounds that, *inter alia*, it amounts to an abandonment of legal principle which will serve to increase uncertainty in the law'. We did, however, also point out that this two-stage approach did 'enable students to understand more readily the subject, than is the case when they have to grapple with principles and decisions which are distorted by unexpressed policy considerations'.

Despite the fact that the dictum of Lord Wilberforce has been applied in numerous subsequent cases, including by the House of Lords in *Junior Books Ltd v Veitchi Co. Ltd* [1982] 3 All ER 201, that criticism has now manifested itself in a considerable reaction against its application. The reasons behind this reaction appear to be as follows.

The potential for expanding the boundaries of negligence which is inherent in the approach of Lord Wilberforce is perhaps self-evident, and that expansion might arise not merely from the recognition of a duty of care in novel situations, but might also be brought about by a disregard of precedents which establish fundamental restrictions on the foreseeability principle. The use of the two-stage approach to that effect was found to be unacceptable; see *Leigh and Sillavan Ltd* v *Aliakmon Shipping Co. Ltd (The Aliakmon)* [1986] 2 All ER 145, HL per Lord Brandon at p. 154:

> I do not think that Lord Wilberforce, in formulating the two questions which he did formulate in his speech in the *Anns* case, was intending them to be used as a means of reopening issues relating to the existence of a duty of care long settled by past decisions.

One important effect of the two-stage approach is that as a result of the presumption of the existence of a prima facie duty of care, based simply on the foreseeability of harm as between the plaintiff and the defendant, a burden is placed on the court to invoke some limitation on policy grounds to justify the adherence to those existing authorities which place some restriction on the foreseeability principle. Whilst the mere foreseeability of harm may of itself be sufficient in some cases to establish the degree of proximity necessary to found a duty of care, it is clearly insufficient in a number of important and sensitive areas. So much has been recognised by Lord Wilberforce himself in the context of injury sustained through shock; see *McLoughlin* v *O'Brian* [1983] 1 AC 410 at p. 421. To apply the 'Wilberforce' approach to these situations would require the courts, on numerous occasions, to justify the status quo (and to deny liability where the harm is merely foreseeable) by reference to policy considerations at the second stage. The prospect of deciding cases (or defending precedent) upon openly stated policy grounds is not one which is relished by many members of the superior courts. Lord Scarman in *McLoughlin* (above) at pp. 429-31, went so far as to suggest that policy matters were 'not justiciable'.

Students may be familiar with the criticisms voiced by Smith and Burns in (1983) 46 MLR 147: '*Donogbue* v *Stevenson* — The Not So Golden Anniversary', that the two-stage approach appears to disregard the well-established distinction drawn between omissions (nonfeasance) and positive acts (misfeasance). This is a good illustration of the kind of difficulty to which we refer above. The judicial disquiet in this respect was later reflected in the judgment of Lord Keith in the decision in *Yuen Kun-yeu* v *Attorney-General of Hong Kong* [1987] 2 All ER 705 at p. 710, where his Lordship took the view that if foreseeability of harm alone created a duty of care, 'there would be liability in negligence on the part of one who sees another about to walk over a cliff with his head in the air and forbears to shout a warning'.

There has been recently a marked reluctance to accept Lord Wilberforce's formulation as authority for the proposition that the mere foreseeability of harm creates even a prima facie duty of care. Students should be aware that many of the cases in which this reluctance has manifested itself have been concerned with claims involving economic loss or the alleged negligent exercise of statutory powers. Two cases in particular are worthy of mention, although they will be discussed in chapters 7 and 9 in a little more depth. In *Caparo* v *Dickman* [1990] 2 WLR 358 and *Murphy* v *Brentwood DC* [1990] 3 WLR 414, the House of Lords has once again commented adversely upon the two-stage approach.

What appears to be a substantial change in the pace of the development of the law of negligence has been achieved in two ways. First, the Privy Council in *Yuen Kun-yeu* (above) interpreted Lord Wilberforce's reference to 'proximity or neighbourhood' (sufficient to give rise to a prima facie duty under his first stage) to be a composite notion 'importing the whole concept of the necessary relationship' between the parties (see [1987] 2 All ER 705 at p. 710). Thus at stage one the court must consider whether *in all the circumstances a duty ought to exist;* the mere foreseeability of harm may not of itself be sufficient. The degree of control which the defendants could exercise, and the purpose of statutory powers given to them were both regarded as essential to the question of the existence of a prima facie duty in *Yuen Kun-yeu* (above) and in *Curran* v *Northern Ireland Co-ownership Housing Association Ltd* [1987] 2 All ER 13, HL. In both cases it was held that no duty of care was owed by the defendants to the plaintiffs. This notion of the requirement of 'proximity' has been reinforced in both *Caparo* (above) and *Murphy* (above) (see Lord Bridge in *Caparo* at p. 368 and Lord Oliver at p. 369). This approach is not without its critics and in an interesting and provocative article, 'Negligence after *Murphy*: Time to Rethink' (1991) 50 CLJ 58, Howarth talks of Lord Keith's 'three-pronged fork', the middle prong now being the convenient concept of 'proximity'.

We also need to remind ourselves of the 'renewed' importance attached to precedent by the House of Lords in *The Aliakmon* (above), which will inevitably place a brake on developments, though the precise effect will no doubt depend upon the willingness of the lower courts to distinguish what would otherwise be binding authorities. This has been reinforced by Lord Oliver (at p. 381):

> Perhaps ... the most that can be attempted is a broad categorisation of the decided cases according to the type of situation in which liability has been established in the past in order to found an argument by analogy.

Howarth is extremely critical of both the 'proximity' concept and argument by analogy process (above at p. 60):

> What the 'proximity concept' and analogical reasoning have in common is that they both allow judges to avoid committing themselves. Since nobody can say what 'proximity' means, it can be asserted in every case to require whatever result is convenient. Similarly, analogies can be accepted as appropriate or rejected as 'unhelpful' as the need arises.

Furthermore, the House of Lords has added what appears to be an additional pre-condition to the existence of a prima facie duty of care, namely that it must be just and reasonable to impose such a duty on the defendant: see *Governors of the Peabody Donation Fund* v *Sir Lindsay Parkinson & Co. Ltd* [1984] 3 WLR 953, HL; *Hill* v *Chief Constable of West Yorkshire* [1988] 2 All ER 238, HL. In reality this requirement appears to be nothing more than a policy of expediency in thin disguise, well illustrated by the recent decision in *Business Computers International Ltd* v *The Registrar of Companies* [1987] 3 All ER 465. In the light of these developments, which now impose a much more demanding test for the existence of a prima facie duty at stage one of the two-stage approach, 'the second stage of Lord Wilberforce's test is one which will rarely have to be applied' (per Lord Keith in *Yuen Kun-yeu* (above) at p. 712).

One other recent decision of the House of Lords deserves mention here; it is that in the case of *Smith* v *Littlewoods Organisation Ltd* [1987] 1 All ER 710. Like the case of *Hill* v *Chief Constable of West Yorkshire* (above), the case takes us into the difficult area of omissions or nonfeasance and raises the question as to circumstances (if any) in which one person may owe a duty of care to act positively to prevent harm being done to the plaintiff by a third person. These cases may also raise issues of causation and remoteness of damage where, for example, it may be argued that a subsequent tortious act of another person severed the causal link between the defendant's alleged negligence and the plaintiff's loss. These cases, such as *Perl (P) (Exporters) Ltd* v *Camden London Borough Council* [1983] 3 All ER 161, and more recently *Topp* v *London Country Bus (South West) Ltd* [1993] 3 All ER 448 are considered in chapter 6.

Students will no doubt be aware that there is no general duty to act positively to protect others in the law of negligence. There are, however, well-established exceptions to that general proposition, illustrated by decisions such as *Home Office* v *Dorset Yacht Co. Ltd* [1970] AC 1004; *Goldman* v *Hargrave* [1967] 1 AC 645. The decision in *Littlewoods* (above) usefully demonstrates the difficulties in formulating satisfactorily an acceptable principle. Though the members of the House of Lords were unanimous in their conclusion that the defendant occupier owed no duty to the plaintiffs, there were substantial differences in the way in which the relevant principle should be expressed.

Students should realise the importance of the recent cases concerning the duty of care mentioned above, for your examiner may well be very interested in testing your understanding of them.

Duty in fact
The relationship between the theoretical duty (duty in law) and a duty in fact is a source of some confusion to students. The phrase 'duty in fact' simply means that in the circumstances of the individual case the type of harm caused to the particular plaintiff by the particular defendant can be shown, on a balance of probabilities, to be reasonably foreseeable. A court's decision on this issue is in effect the second stage of the judicial process, the first being to decide whether or not a theoretical duty exists or should exist. The order of the process is then as follows:

Stage 1 — Is there, or should there be a duty in law to exercise reasonable care by, e.g., manufacturers, to avoid foreseeable harm to consumers? Assuming that this question is answered in the affirmative, as indeed it was in *Donoghue* v *Stevenson* [1932] AC 562 (there being in the majority view no policy consideration sufficient to justify the denial of that duty), then:

Stage 2 — Was the type of harm caused, e.g., to the plaintiff in the above case by the defendant manufacturer of the ginger-beer, reasonably foreseeable on the facts?

The House of Lords, in *Donoghue* v *Stevenson*, was not called upon to decide this latter question since the sole ground of appeal in that case was on the question as to whether there existed a duty of care in law. In so far as the issue of duty in fact was to be the subject of litigation, that was a matter for the court of first instance. A plaintiff may well succeed in establishing a duty on the facts, but his success should not be taken for granted. It is by no means beyond the bounds of possibility that a court might view the established facts through 'policy spectacles' and interpret the facts against the plaintiff. Whilst the decision in *Bourhill* v *Young* [1943] AC 92 is perhaps a good illustration, that was after all a decision of the House of Lords. It is unlikely that a lower court would adopt such a view following the decision of an appellate court that a duty of care in law existed particularly in a novel case. Settlement out of court is probably far more likely as reputedly happened following the decision by their lordships in *Donoghue* v *Stevenson*. (The claim was apparently settled for £100.)

The practice of raising before a court, either at first instance or on appeal, the single question of the existence of a notional duty, is now well established. The decision in *Anns* v *Merton London Borough Council* [1978] AC 728 was a more recent example of that practice which is a practical manifestation of the theoretical exercise. Students often fail to appreciate that a court is in these cases being called upon only to decide whether a duty in law does or should exist and wrongly equate an affirmative decision on that issue with a finding of liability.

ILLUSTRATIVE QUESTION

'That foreseeability does not of itself ... automatically lead to a duty of care is, I think clear' (per Lord Wilberforce). Discuss.

COMMENTARY ON EXAMINATION TECHNIQUE AND SUBSTANTIVE ISSUES

In our experience many students do not perform particularly well when answering a question of this type on the notional duty of care. This is due, at least in part, to the fact that a good number of students never quite understand the concept and its relationship with other aspects of the tort. As we pointed out in chapter 2 such topics are popular with examiners for this very reason.

There is, however, another, equally common, reason why students obtain fairly mediocre marks on this type of question. It is that many of them seem to have little idea as to how to approach such a question and demonstrate woefully inadequate examination technique. The question clearly invites students to discuss the relevance of policy considerations in the formulation of the notional duty of care. There is, as we are all well aware, a significant number of areas where the notional duty is negated or in some way restricted on policy grounds. There is available, therefore, such a quantity of relevant material that it cannot all be deployed in the time available except in a fashion which is likely to be superficial and descriptive. Whilst such an approach may gain a pass mark, a much more selective approach creates the opportunity to demonstrate a level of knowledge and understanding which will be rewarded with a substantially higher mark. We would advise students therefore to be bold, imaginative and selective! You should inform the examiner in your answer that you have adopted such an approach and why.

Choose no more than two areas of law to discuss, for example, nervous shock and advocate's immunity, in which the respective policy considerations differ (there are, after all, considerations of policy other than the fear of 'indeterminate liability'). In an examination it would be sensible to choose those areas in which you feel that you have greatest knowledge.

If you lack the self-confidence to adopt such an approach (or if you only possess a depth of knowledge in one area of law) then a perfectly acceptable compromise can be struck between the two above-mentioned approaches. The earlier part of your answer can be devoted to what might be described as a general review of a number of areas in which the notional duty is affected by considerations of policy and the latter part of your answer can be concerned with a more detailed study of one such area. The following commentary is based on the assumption that this latter approach is to be adopted. In our view an answer could be sensibly structured along the following lines.

First, explain in a clear and concise fashion, the function of the notional duty and the associated difficulties. The second part of your answer should then contain a general review of the main areas of law in which policy considerations affect the notional duty. The third section can then be devoted to a more detailed discussion of one of these areas (we offer some guidance below as to the depth of discussion students should seek to achieve in this part of their answer). The answer itself should then be rounded off with a conclusion which draws together the main points. The substantive and conceptual issues with which students are likely to find difficulty will arise under the first and third parts of the answer and our later commentary is largely confined to those issues.

Before turning to those matters it is perhaps worth while to remind students to produce a very brief rough plan which reflects the structure of their answer and sets out in note form the main areas to be reviewed in the second part of the answer together with the relevant policy considerations and cases. It would be useful to include a heading such as 'novel cases' to remind you of any recently decided cases, some mention of which in your answer should surely cause the examiner to swoon with delight. The plan should also include, in similar fashion, a list of the more detailed points to be made in the third part of the answer. The use of a rough plan in connection with an essay-type question is likely to lead to the production of an answer which is better structured and more balanced than would otherwise be the case.

The Substantive and Conceptual Issues

(a) As we indicated earlier the question of the existence of a notional duty of care in the tort of negligence, its relationship with both duty in fact and breach of that duty often perplexes students. It follows that an examiner would be suitably impressed if a student is able to give, albeit somewhat briefly, some indication of understanding the issue. The deliberately simplified explanation which follows will hopefully assist students in that respect.

The question at issue is whether in any given factual situation a duty of care is in law capable of existing. Had subsequent decisions accepted literally Lord Atkin's dictum in *Donoghue* v *Stevenson* [1932] AC 562 at p. 580, that foreseeability of harm itself created such a duty, then the question would of course be entirely superfluous today. Courts would simply consider the evidence in any particular case to decide if on the established facts D had caused a foreseeable type of harm to P. In so doing the court would not only decide whether a duty in fact existed, but also whether a breach of that duty had occurred and whether the damage was too remote. In short, the infliction by D of a particular type of harm upon P, which was on the facts foreseeable, would almost automatically result in liability.

The sheer scale of litigation and the level of redistribution of losses which such a position might well entail was in the past wholly unacceptable to the judicial mind. To apply, unrestrained, the foreseeability principle in the words of Cardozo CJ would impose 'liability in an indeterminate amount for an indeterminate time to an indeterminate class' (*Ultramares Corporation* v *Touche* (1931) 174 NE 441 at p. 44). Thus, 'In order to limit liability ... courts sometimes say either that the damage claimed was "too remote" or that it was not "caused" by the defendant's carelessness ... or that the defendant did not "owe a duty of care" to the plaintiff' (per Thesiger in *SCM (United Kingdom) Ltd* v *W. J. Whittall & Son Ltd* [1970] 1 WLR 1017, at p. 1031).

In the past 20 years or so we have witnessed two interrelated developments. The first is the more open acknowledgement of the relevance of policy considerations. This has to some extent occurred by way of a reaction against the conceptual confusion which has been created by the attempts to accommodate the restrictions which the courts perceived as being necessary (see, for example, Lord Denning MR in *Spartan Steel & Alloys Ltd* v *Martin & Co. (Contractors) Ltd* [1973] QB 27). In addition the tort of negligence has until recently continued its relentless expansion. The courts had shown themselves to be increasingly willing to loosen the fetters on the foreseeability principle and more reluctant to accept the 'indeterminate liability' argument. Indeed that argument has, at least theoretically, been turned against its advocates — if negligent behaviour adversely effects the interests of large numbers of people, that may be a factor in favour of the creation of liability. The position was reached where it was legitimate to ask whether there was at least a presumption that foreseeability of harm created a duty in law. That question was answered in the affirmative by Lord Reid in *Home Office* v *Dorset Yacht Co. Ltd* [1970] AC 1004 at p. 1027 and affirmed by the House of Lords in *Anns* v *Merton London Borough Council* [1978] AC 728. That presumption is encapsulated in Lord Wilberforce's two-stage approach (which we discussed earlier), the application of which led to a degree of expansion in the law of negligence, in some cases at the expense of precedent, see for example *The Irene's Success* [1982] QB 481, now expressly overruled in *The Aliakmon* (above). This expansionist trend perhaps reached its high water mark in *Junior Books Ltd* v *Veitchi Co. Ltd* [1982] 3 All ER 201 and is clearly now on the wane in the light of *Caparo* (above) and *Murphy* (above).

It is particularly important in addressing the question that students show an appreciation of the fact that a substantial modification of that approach has taken place. This will necessitate some discussion of cases such as *Yuen Kun-Yeu, The Aliakmon, Curran, Hill, Caparo, Murphy*, etc., the effect of which we considered in the earlier part of this chapter. Given the number of important cases which reflect this change, it would not be sensible, in the time available in an examination, to give a detailed account of all of them. One way of resolving this difficulty is perhaps to refer to them by name, indicating whether they are decisions of the House of Lords, Privy Council, Court of Appeal, etc., and to support that opinion by using a relatively brief quotation from one of the authoritative judgments in the case.

In recognising the cautious incremental approach to novel cases now advocated by the House of Lords, a student ought to give some indication of the considerations which may affect the outcome of such cases. These considerations may well be invoked in order to deny the existence of a duty of care notwithstanding a high degree of proximity between plaintiff and defendant. These would for example include:

(i)   The potential impact upon some other established area of law (contract law, see *D & F Estates Ltd* v *Church Commissioners* [1988] 2 All ER 992, HL) (defamation, see *Spring* v *Guardian Assurance plc* [1993] 2 All ER 273, CA cf [1994] 3 WLR 354, HL).

(ii)   Whether an alternative remedy existed (see *James* v *Department of Employment* [1988] 1 All ER 725) or an alternative source of compensation existed (see *Hill* v *Chief Constable of West Yorkshire* [1988] 2 All ER 238).

(iii)   A duty is unlikely to be recognised if this might adversely interfere with the exercise of discretion or judgment (see *Hill* v *Chief Constable of West Yorkshire* (above)).

(b)   In the second part of the answer when reviewing the main areas in which the notional duty is negated or restricted by considerations of policy, that review should include an outline of the major cases and the specific restrictions they impose in such areas as nervous shock, economic loss, exercise of statutory powers, advocate's immunity and omissions. Obviously one should make a special effort to mention recent cases of any importance or interest and offer some meaningful comment upon them. Merely making mention of them in a sort of 'make weight' fashion with no evaluation will do little to impress your examiner. In the area of economic loss, for example, in addition to the cases mentioned above, one could usefully include some observations upon the very interesting decisions in *Spring* v *Guardian Assurance* [1993] above; *White* v *Jones* [1993] 3 All ER 481, (1995) *The Times*, 17 February. Two other decisions in this area illustrate very well what may be regarded as a retreat from the 'high water' mark of *Junior Books*. In both cases *Junior Books* was distinguished and its impact confined: see *Simaan General Contracting Co.* v *Pilkington Glass Ltd (No. 2)* [1988] 1 All ER 791, CA; *Greater Nottingham Cooperative Society* v *Cementation Piling and Foundations Ltd* [1988] 2 All ER 971.

The decision in *Alexandrou* v *Oxford* [1993] 4 All ER 328, CA; *Ancell* v *McDermott* [1993] 4 All ER 355, CA and *Osmond* v *Ferguson* [1994] 4 All ER 344 demonstrate that the reluctance to impose any duty of care upon the police extends far beyond the problem of the failure to apprehend criminals, illustrated in *Hill* v *Chief Constable of West Yorkshire* (above).

In the area of nervous shock the decision of the Court of Appeal in *Attia* v *British Gas plc* [1987] 3 All ER 455, in which the court refused to strike out a claim for shock sustained by the plaintiff at the sight of damage to his property, is an obvious candidate for inclusion. One would also very much hope to see expressed the thoughts of the student as to possible scope of liability in cases of this kind. 'Nervous shock' was perhaps, until recently, the one area where the expansionist trend in favour of liability seemed not to have been curtailed. This will be discussed in more depth in chapter 8.

As to negligent exercise of statutory powers, the more recent decisions in *Yuen Kun-yeu* and *Curran* (above) are of similar importance, for they both demonstrate that the purpose of the statutory powers in question and the degree of control which they give to the defendant may be crucial factors in determining whether or not even a prima facie duty of care is owed. These two cases, together with the most recent pronouncements of the Privy Council in *Rowling* v *Takaro Properties Ltd* [1988] 1 All ER 163, are excellent illustrations of the disfavour with which Lord Wilberforce's dictum in *Anns* is currently viewed. The decision in *Rowling* is also important in view of the fact that the Privy Council made some interesting observations on the distinction to be drawn between policy decisions and operational decisions, a point which Lord Wilberforce made in *Anns*. In addition, of course, the departure from the decision in *Anns* v *Merton* in *Murphy* possibly constitutes the death knell for this category of development in negligence.

There appear to have been no recent decisions which disregard the fundamental distinction between misfeasance and nonfeasance (pure omission) despite the invitation to do so which, it has been argued, is implicit in the now discredited two-stage approach. Nevertheless, one might reasonably expect to see some evaluation of the criticisms by Smith and Burns, 'Donoghue v Stevenson — The Not So Golden Anniversary' (1983) 46 MLR 147. Recent cases in this area which would merit some observation from the student are Smith v Littlewoods Organisation Ltd [1987] 1 All ER 710, King v Liverpool City Council [1986] 3 All ER 544, CA and Topp v London Country Bus (South West) Ltd (above). The first two cases are concerned with the circumstances in which, if any, an occupier owes a duty to act positively to prevent foreseeable damage to the plaintiff resulting from a danger created by the actions of vandals. In both cases the court took the view that no duty of care was owed. On the facts, neither fell within the special circumstances in which such a duty had been recognised by earlier authorities. As mentioned previously, however, the two cases do demonstrate rather well the difficulties which the courts continue to experience in their attempts to formulate principles which are regarded as appropriate to this issue.

(c)   We suggested that in the third part of the answer to the above question it might be wise to seek to demonstrate some depth of knowledge albeit with regard to one relatively narrow area of law. In order to impress the examiner students need to appreciate what is likely to be expected of them in this respect and how those expectations might be satisfied in the most efficient manner, given the constraint of time and the amount of material which may be relevant. In our view students would be well advised to bear in mind the following basic points.

Having chosen an area in which the notional duty of care is to some degree excluded or restricted, a student should attempt to state what the law is or is thought to be. This will obviously include a review of cases which have accepted or rejected the existence of the notional duty on particular facts. The student should, however, be concerned to convey to the examiner an understanding of any uncertainty in the law. Thus, for example, a student should make a point of mentioning any cases in which a court has adverted to the effect of its decision in other fact situations but has expressly reserved its position in that respect. A student should also identify and explain the relevant policy considerations which have led the courts to deny, or in some way restrict, the notional duty of care. Furthermore, it is not merely desirable but necessary that a student should question whether the restrictions imposed are consistent with those policy considerations.

In dealing with these matters a student should demonstrate that he is conversant not only with the leading authorities which are relevant, but also with any major differences of judicial opinion which may have been expressed in dissenting judgments and indeed any differences in reasoning underlying the majority views in the Court of Appeal or House of Lords. The student could also usefully refer to any criticisms in the academic journals and should be prepared to evaluate such criticism and state his own position.

To achieve all that in what is, after all, only a part of your answer may appear to be rather more than a tall order. May we offer a few words of encouragement. By attempting greater depth in this part of the answer you are seeking to persuade the examiner to give a higher mark than he would otherwise give. The examiner will treat any such attempt with a good deal of respect even though it falls far short of perfection. The area you have chosen to discuss should be one in which you are most knowledgeable. Students would perhaps welcome some reassurance as to the level of discussion which they might reasonably expect to achieve in the time available. In order to give guidance on this we have outlined below the kind of points which we would regard as being important in a discussion of the duty of care owed by legal advisers and advocates.

By way of brief introduction it would be useful to state the law prior to 1964, namely, that due to the absence of any contractual relationship between barrister and client the former enjoyed immunity from any action based on negligence whether the alleged negligence arose out of advocacy or work unconnected with litigation, the exact reverse being true with regard to solicitors.

That position was brought into question by the decision of the House of Lords in *Hedley Byrne & Co. Ltd* v *Heller & Partners Ltd* [1964] AC 465 in which it was held that a duty of reasonable care in law could exist within a special relationship (which was neither contractual nor fiduciary) with regard to pure financial loss.

The decision in *Hedley Byrne* was used to challenge the barrister's immunity in *Rondel* v *Worsley* [1969] 1 AC 191. The action arose from the alleged negligence of the defendant barrister in the conduct of the defence in a criminal trial. The plaintiff's claim was regarded as being particularly weak in that the work had been undertaken under the old dock brief system and the action was commenced more than five years after the date of the criminal trial. The sole question before the court was whether a barrister did or could owe a duty of care in law with regard to the conduct of the case in court. Whilst recognising that foreseeable harm could result to clients in the event of negligence on the part of a barrister, the House of Lords held that no such duty should exist in relation to advocacy or preliminary work connected with the conduct of the case in court. Their lordships justified their conclusion on three grounds of policy:

(i)   The administration of justice required that a barrister should be free to discharge his duty to the court without fear of actions by disgruntled clients.

(ii)   The difficulties in effect of retrying the original action and prolonging litigation which would be contrary to the public interest.

(iii)   The barrister under the cab-rank rule was obliged to accept any client, no matter how difficult, who sought his services.

The majority were of the opinion, however, that those considerations did not require that a barrister be immune from an action in negligence with regard to work unconnected with litigation. There were also strong *obiter* suggestions to the effect that solicitors enjoyed the same degree of immunity.

The conclusion of the House of Lords differed substantially from that of the Court of Appeal [1967] 1 QB 443. Though there was little difference of opinion as to the relevant policy considerations, the majority in the Court of Appeal (Lord Denning MR, Danckwerts LJ) had been prepared to uphold the previous position whereby barristers enjoyed a total immunity and solicitors none. The decision of the Court of Appeal can be legitimately criticised in this respect. How is the administration of justice only impeded where the advocate open to an action in negligence is a barrister as opposed to a solicitor?

The later decision of the House of Lords in *Saif Ali* v *Sydney Mitchell & Co.* [1980] AC 198 to some extent clarified the law. As a result a duty of care in law may be owed by both solicitors and barristers with regard to work unconnected with litigation. However, neither owes any such duty with regard to the conduct of a case in court or in respect of pre-trial work which is intimately connected with the conduct of the case in court.

Future difficulties would seem to lie in deciding whether or not pre-trial work falls within or is without the immunity, a point well illustrated in *Saif Ali* itself. The House of Lords, by a majority of 3–2 held that the failure to issue writs against the appropriate persons within the limitation period fell outside the area of immunity. Lord Salmon took the view that the alleged negligence was 'not even remotely connected with counsel's duty to the court or with public policy', whilst in the Court of Appeal (the decision of which was reversed by the House) the opposite view had been taken.

The majority of their lordships in *Saif Ali* expressed forcefully the view that the protection afforded in respect of pre-trial work should be no wider than is absolutely necessary in the interests of the administration of justice. Adherence to that view in subsequent cases is likely to cause defendant barristers and solicitors more than a little difficulty in persuading a court that they owe no duty of care to their clients in respect of pre-trial work. That such adherence will be forthcoming in future cases may be somewhat speculative, however, in the light of the considerable differences of judicial opinion so far demonstrated.

Our caution in expressing this view is perhaps now justified in the light of the most recent decision of the Court of Appeal in *Somasunderam* v *M. Julius Melchior & Co.* [1989] 1 All ER 129. The case concerned an allegation of negligence by the plaintiff against both his solicitor and counsel in advising him to plead guilty to a charge of malicious wounding for which he received a prison sentence on conviction. Whilst the appellant's claim was dismissed on the grounds that, in the absence of any evidence of negligence the claim was both frivolous and vexatious, the court expressed some very interesting views as to the law. In so doing the court has considerably widened the immunity of both solicitors and barristers beyond that recognised in *Rondel* and *Saif Ali*. Students need to show an awareness of the fact that this has been achieved through the adoption of the quite separate doctrine of abuse of legal process. Thus, even though the barrister has no immunity under *Saif Ali*, nevertheless, where a civil action against him would have the effect, directly or indirectly, of impugning a final decision of a criminal court, public policy requires that such action should not be permitted: see *Hunter* v *Chief Constable of West Midlands* [1982] AC 529.

The Court of Appeal in *Somasunderam* (above) was concerned not to extend the immunity of solicitors and barristers as advocates under *Saif Ali* any further than was absolutely necessary in the interests of justice, and expressly ruled that immunity on this basis was not on the facts a ground for striking out the action. The decision in *Somasunderam* is quite clearly an important one and students hoping for a decent mark would need to show the kind of understanding of the case indicated above. Obviously any further critical analysis of the present position would be suitably rewarded. In order to be in a position to offer such an answer the student needs to have formed a critical view long before the examination.

In writing a conclusion to their answer students might, in view of the above commentary, state their agreement with Lord Wilberforce's proposition quoted in our illustrative question. In so doing, it would be sensible to emphasise that the notional duty of care remains an important control device, but the trend in recent cases has been to reject the notion that mere foreseeability of harm is sufficient to establish the requisite degree of proximity, a trend which actually supports the view expressed by Lord Wilberforce in his judgment in *McLoughlin* v *O'Brian* (above) from which the proposition was actually taken. It also seems clear that the present House of Lords prefers the cautious, incremental argument by analogy approach to any expansion of the duty concept, fearing the danger of the broad general principle approach seen to be inherent in the *Anns* two-stage approach.

SELECTED READING

Howarth, 'Negligence After Murphy: Time to Rethink' [1991] CLJ 58.

Markesinis and Deakin, 'The Random Element in their Lordship's Infallible Judgment' (1992) 55 MLR 619.

Smith and Burns, '*Donoghue* v *Stevenson*: The Not So Golden Anniversary' (1983) 46 MLR 147.

Symmons, 'The Duty of Care in Negligence: Recently Expressed Policy Elements' (1971) 34 MLR 394.

5 NEGLIGENCE 2: BREACH OF DUTY AND BURDEN OF PROOF

INTRODUCTION

Assuming that the plaintiff has established that the defendant owed him a duty of care in law and on the facts of the particular case, he is required to show, on the balance of probabilities, that the defendant is in breach of that duty. Breach of duty and proof are inextricably bound together and for that reason we have included consideration of the issue of the burden of proof in this chapter. In particular, we shall examine the scope of the maxim *'res ipsa loquitur'* (the thing speaks for itself).

As we shall see below, breach of the duty of care is a mixed question of fact and law. In practice few cases raise issues solely of law, consequently many of the cases have little precedent value. Acquiring a knowledge of a vast number of cases, as such, will not necessarily advance the student's understanding of the breach-of-duty issue. Selectivity is perhaps important in this respect. Students should concentrate upon those cases which give an indication as to the relevant factors which the courts take into account and which also are clear illustrations of the application of those factors. We have tried to demonstrate this by our choice of relevant cases later in this chapter.

From an examination point of view the issues of breach and burden of proof may be examined singly or together by means of either an essay question or as part of a problem-type question. In this chapter we have chosen to adopt an essay-style question. However, in chapter 6, on causation and remoteness of damage, the problem question also contains points relating to breach and the burden of proof.

SUBSTANTIVE DIFFICULTIES

Relationship Between Duty in Fact and Breach

It is sometimes said that foreseeability of the type of harm sustained by the plaintiff in effect decides both the issue of duty in fact and breach of that duty. This is a misleading oversimplification. It must be recognised that there are two different aspects to the issue of duty in fact, namely, (a) the existence of such a duty and (b) the extent of that duty. Questions associated with breach are concerned with the latter aspect. Foreseeability of the type of harm a plaintiff sustained is certainly relevant in deciding the issue of breach, but it is not the sole measure of the defendant's conduct. A finding that harm is foreseeable identifies a certain degree of probability of risk of harm to the particular plaintiff, but does not measure the defendant's conduct as such. In this respect the law requires the defendant to exercise reasonable care, that is, to take such care as is reasonable in all the circumstances. If a court concludes that a defendant has exercised reasonable care, then he will not be liable to the plaintiff, notwithstanding the fact he has caused the latter foreseeable harm. However, it is perhaps worth emphasising that the extent to which harm is foreseeable may well affect the degree of care which the defendant is required to exercise.

Standard of Care

This leads us to ask what standard of care is required by the law of persons generally. There are two issues which cause students considerable difficulty in this context. The first is the suggestion that as a matter of law there exists a single, objective standard of care with which all persons must comply. (See Megaw LJ in *Nettleship* v *Weston* [1971] 2 QB 691 at pp. 707-9.) Statements such as the standard is that of 'the man on the Clapham omnibus' lead students to believe that there is one such single standard, which ignores such factors as the skill, knowledge, age and disability of the individual defendant. Yet precisely these factors are taken into account in the cases (see, e.g., *Wells* v *Cooper* [1958] 2 QB 265). How can this apparent conflict be reconciled?

The second issue with which students find difficulty concerns the relevance of certain factors identified in the decided cases. In deciding whether the defendant has exercised reasonable care in all the circumstances the courts take account of such factors as the degree of probability of harm, the seriousness of the likely harm, the social utility of the defendant's conduct and so on. The problem for students lies not in the identification of the relevant factors but in recognising the appropriate weighting which may be given to each or any of them in any particular decision.

Policy Considerations

The difficulty which students experience when attributing appropriate weighting to the factors mentioned above may stem often from the failure to recognise the influence of policy considerations. That influence may well explain the apparent discrepancies in what is perceived to be a failure to exercise reasonable care. Perhaps the most obvious example which highlights this inconsistency is the comparison between the standard of care expected of drivers of motor vehicles and that expected of the medical profession. A momentary lapse of attention by a car driver or a doctor may be regarded in a totally different light, reflecting possibly the issues such as the availability of insurance and the prospect of defensive medicine.

Burden of Proof

There seems to be a number of issues on the burden of proof which students find difficult to grasp. The first of these occurs in what might be termed the normal case where the burden of proof lies with the plaintiff. Students often fail to appreciate the distinction between 'primary' facts and 'secondary' or 'inferred' facts. A finding of negligence is a process of inference from primary facts. In many cases there is obviously uncertainty in predicting in advance whether a court will draw such an inference. There is a further aspect to this concerning an appellate court's authority and indeed willingness to disturb not only the findings of primary facts but also the inferences drawn from the facts by the court of first instance. That is not to say that an appellate court will refrain from this step in an appropriate case (see, for example, *Whitehouse* v *Jordan* [1981] 1 WLR 246).

Students also experience difficulty with the application and effect of the maxim *'res ipsa loquitur'*. No doubt these difficulties result from the apparently haphazard fashion in which the maxim is employed in the cases. There is also some confusion, amongst both academics and the judiciary, as to whether the application of the maxim places a legal or merely an evidentiary burden of proof on the defendant. It may well be that in practice this distinction may be of little or no significance.

A number of recent cases have illustrated the difficulties which a plaintiff may experience in seeking to prove that the defendant's breach of duty was a cause in fact of his (the plaintiff's) harm: see *Hotson* v *East Berkshire Area Health Authority* [1987] 2 All ER 909; *Kay* v *Ayrshire and Arran Health Board* [1987] 2 All ER 417; *Wilsher* v *Essex Area Health Authority* [1988] 1 All ER 871; *Fitzgerald* v *Lane* [1988] 3 WLR 356. These and other cases are considered in chapter 6.

ILLUSTRATIVE QUESTION

'The standard of foresight of the reasonable man is, in one sense, an impersonal test. It eliminates the personal equation and is independent of the idiosyncrasies of the particular person whose conduct is in question.' (Per Lord Macmillan in *Glasgow Corporation* v *Muir* [1943] AC 448 at p. 457.) Discuss.

COMMENTARY

Introduction

Unlike the illustrative essay question in the previous chapter, the above quotation should cause few difficulties of technique for the student, but it is still worth while drafting a rough plan of an answer. The major difficulty with this question may well lie in the selection of appropriate material in view of the vast number of cases on the issue of breach of duty. Students should also remember to respond to the quotation in a positive manner. Does the proposition by Lord Macmillan accurately reflect the case law or to what extent does it need to be qualified? There seem to be three possible qualifications to the quotation. The first concerns his lordship's use of the word 'foresight' as opposed to 'foreseeability'. As is pointed out in *Clerk and Lindsell on Torts* (16th ed., p. 576) it is important to realise that the test is what the courts deem to have been reasonably foreseeable in the circumstances, i.e., hindsight, not foresight (see also Lord Wilberforce in *McLougblin* v *O'Brian* [1983] 1 AC 410 at pp. 420-1). Clearly, any test based upon foreseeability is likely to require a defendant to guard against a wider range of risks than may have been foreseen at the time. However, a word of caution must be entered here. A defendant is only to be judged in the light of the current state of actual knowledge at the time of the alleged negligence, a point which will be more fully developed later in this discussion. To this extent Lord Macmillan's dictum perhaps understates the scope of potential liability. Whether we use, as Lord Macmillan did, the word 'foresight', or as we prefer the word 'foreseeability', a further qualification lies in the fact that the dictum focuses on this aspect only. As we pointed out earlier 'foreseeability' is not the sole measure of the defendant's conduct: other factors are relevant, such as social utility, practicability of precautions and so on, and these require discussion later. Perhaps the most significant qualification to the dictum revolves around the apparent suggestion that there is a single objectively assessed standard of care, which ignores matters such as the defendant's knowledge, skill, age and disability. The above-mentioned qualifications to Lord Macmillan's dictum may be used to provide a structure for the remainder of your answer. We need say no more about the distinction between foresight and foreseeability and now direct our comments to the last two qualifications which are arguably more important.

Qualifications to the Dictum

Both these qualifications are concerned with the standard of care in law and its application to the facts of individual cases. It seems proper to start with the oft-quoted statement of principle in *Blyth* v *Birmingham Waterworks Co.* (1856) 11 Exch 781 at p. 784 to the effect that negligence, in the sense of a breach of the duty of care 'is the omission to do something which a reasonable man, guided upon those considerations which ordinarily regulate the conduct of human affairs, would do, or doing something which a prudent and reasonable man would not do'.

The broad generality of this statement is strikingly obvious. What is perhaps not so obvious, because it is couched in terms conveying objectivity, is that the concept of the reasonable man may be nothing more than a vehicle for the subjective opinions of individual judges. It is through this central concept that policy considerations are translated into legal decisions.

The question arises as to how the courts apply such a broad principle in order to decide on the particular facts of cases. There are certain relationships in which the law lays down with some degree of particularity elements comprised in the appropriate standard of care, for example, reasonable care on the part of an employer requires him to provide a safe place of work, safe equipment and so on (see Lord Wright in *Wilsons & Clyde Coal Co. Ltd* v *English* [1938] AC 57 at p. 78). However, in the vast majority of situations the judge must fall back upon factors relating to the likelihood of harm, the seriousness of the harm, the social utility of the defendant's activity, the practicability of precautions, common or customary practice and the state of current knowledge. As we pointed out earlier students may have difficulty in assessing the relative weight to be given to each or any of these factors. This may stem from the uncertainty created by the broad nature of the principle and the importance of the policy considerations. The student who shows an appreciation of this will no doubt score well with the examiner. We would suggest, therefore, that your discussion of the relevant factors should be strongly orientated in this direction.

Relevant Factors

In dealing with the factors mentioned above the student will no doubt have to be selective as far as the case law is concerned. It would make sense to choose the well-known cases which are good illustrations of the way the courts employ the various factors. This should not preclude at least a mention of any recent decisions which are relevant illustrations of the application of these matters, since an examiner is likely to look favourably on the inclusion of such material in an answer.

The following discussion concentrates on the more important of the factors which are omitted from Lord Macmillan's dictum. The probability of harm which might arise from a particular activity is something to which a court will have regard. It is said that the reasonable man guards against a reasonable probability rather than some remote possibility of harm. The degree of risk in *Bolton* v *Stone* [1951] AC 850 fell into the latter category, because the cricket ball had only been struck out of the ground very infrequently and the likelihood of its striking a passer-by was perceived as being very low. It may also be necessary to take account of the seriousness of the type of harm, for it has to be recognised that a low degree of risk may nevertheless result in extremely serious consequences for the individual affected. For example, there might only be a minute degree of risk of escape involved in the manufacture of some useful, but deadly, gas. The seriousness of the consequences, however, of its escape might well outweigh the remote possibility of that escape. Obviously, the cost and practicability of totally eliminating any such risk of escape may need to be taken into account on which we shall say a little more below. The greater seriousness of consequence resulting from a low risk may stem from the plaintiff's own circumstances, for example, in *Paris* v *Stepney Borough Council* [1951] AC 367, where it was recognised that an employer was not justified in ignoring a small degree of risk of harm, and thus failing to provide goggles to an employee whom the employer knew to have only one eye amounted to negligence.

We have already mentioned that a court may have taken into account the cost and practicability of precautions to obviate a risk, when considering the defendant's conduct. A case often cited by way of illustration is the decision of the House of Lords in *Latimer* v *AEC Ltd* [1953] AC 643. In that case the floor of the respondent's factory was rendered slippery by a flood of unprecedented proportions. Whilst considerable efforts were made to reduce the risks through the use of sawdust, the appellant slipped in an area which had not been treated and was injured. At first instance Pilcher J ([1952] 1 All ER 443) found that the respondents had failed to exercise reasonable care on the sole ground that they had not closed down the factory. The House of Lords took quite a different view and held that the evidence as to the degree of risk involved was insufficient to justify such an extreme and costly step. The relevance of this consideration can also be seen in cases where the defendant is found to be negligent. The court may well emphasise how little the defendant need have done in order to obviate the risk which caused harm to the plaintiff, for example, see *Goldman* v *Hargrave* [1967] 1 AC 645 (PC) and *Sedleigh-Denfield* v *O'Callaghan* [1940] AC 880. Whilst the latter is a decision in nuisance, nonetheless it illustrates the relevance of this particular factor and students should not be afraid to employ relevant material in this way.

A further factor mentioned above is that of the social utility of the defendant's activities. As was succinctly stated by Asquith LJ in *Daborn v Bath Tramways Motor Co. Ltd* [1946] 2 All ER 333 at p. 336, 'The purpose to be served, if sufficiently important, justifies the assumption of abnormal risk'.

Thus the use of a left-hand-drive ambulance in an emergency, such as time of war, did not of itself amount to negligence. The student ought to show awareness of the fact that the concept of social utility is a subjective and dynamic notion and individual cases should be treated with some caution. In *Watt v Hertfordshire County Council* [1954] 2 All ER 368 the Court of Appeal took the view that the risk of injury sustained by the plaintiff fireman resulting from the use of an unsuitable vehicle was justified in the circumstances of an attempt to save life and limb. This should not be taken to mean that the taking of *any* risk is warranted in an emergency situation. As Denning LJ pointed out at p. 371: 'I quite agree that fire engines, ambulances and doctors' cars should not shoot past the traffic lights when they show a red light. That is because the risk is too great to warrant the incurring of the danger.'

In addition, in the same case, Denning LJ took the view that risks which might justifiably be run in the pursuit of a humanitarian purpose, as in the case itself, might not be so favourably regarded in the context of a commercial venture. Students should appreciate that this notion of social utility is not confined solely to the tort of negligence, but is also a factor to be found in the tort of nuisance. In view of the overlap between these two torts, there is no reason why the student should not make use of relevant cases from that area.

A further factor to which courts may give consideration is that of common or customary practice within some particular trade, industry or profession. The relevance of this factor is largely evidentiary as was pointed out by Lord Dunedin in *Morton v William Dixon Ltd* 1909 SC 807. His view was that proof of fault should be one of two kinds: 'either — to show that the thing which [the defendant] did not do was a thing which was commonly done by other persons in like circumstances, or — to show that it was a thing which was so obviously wanted that it would be folly in anyone to neglect to provide it'.

Compliance with or deviation from a clearly established practice may have a substantial bearing on the outcome. However, in a number of cases (see, for example, *Cavanagh v Ulster Weaving Co. Ltd* [1960] AC 145) the courts have shown themselves willing to find that even a common or customary practice constituted a failure to take reasonable care. In the context of injuries sustained in the course of medical treatment the issue is particularly problematic. This perhaps stems from the fact that medicine is still an imprecise science and perfectly respectable but conflicting differences of medical opinion may exist on particular issues. The appropriate test in such cases was laid down in *Bolam v Friern Hospital Management Committee* [1957] 1 WLR 582 and has recently been approved at the highest level in *Maynard* v

West Midlands Regional Health Authority [1984] 1 WLR 634 in which Lord Scarman said at p. 638:

> A case which is based on an allegation that a fully considered decision of two consultants in the field of their special skill was negligent clearly presents certain difficulties of proof. It is not enough to show that there is a body of competent professional opinion which considers that theirs was a wrong decision, if there also exists a body of professional opinion, equally competent, which supports the decision as reasonable in the circumstances.

The student might forcefully illustrate the point by drawing the examiner's attention to the conflict of opinion as to the preferable way of restraining patients subjected to electro-convulsive therapy as in the *Bolam* case.

In addition to factors such as the degree of risk and the seriousness of the harm another factor to which brief reference was made earlier and which goes to the issue of foreseeability is that of the current state of knowledge in the particular field at the time of the alleged negligence. This is again, perhaps, best illustrated by a case from the medical sphere, *Roe v Minister of Health* [1954] 2 QB 66. The plaintiff in that case was injured in 1947 as a result of a defect in medical equipment. The defect in question was unknown at that time. The Court of Appeal found the defendants not guilty of negligence, and in his judgment (at p. 84) Denning LJ expressed the view that 'We must not took at the 1947 accident with 1954 spectacles'. Students should be at pains to emphasise, as did Denning LJ in the above case (at p. 86), that once knowledge has been acquired of a particular risk, then reasonable steps will need to be taken to avoid a repetition of such an incident.

Single, Objective Standard of Care?

The third qualification to the dictum of Lord Macmillan, which we suggested above, questions the existence in law of a single objectively assessed standard of care of general application. The existence of such a standard would appear to deny, as does Lord Macmillan, that the law takes account of the individual defendant's skill, knowledge, age or disability. In the following discussion we shall seek to show that these matters are relevant factors in assessing the defendant's conduct. We have not included this under the previous heading, where it might have been appropriate to deal with it, and we have included it here in order to challenge this issue of a single objective standard, perhaps the most difficult topic, from a student viewpoint, on the issue of breach. We shall attempt to demonstrate that, although there may exist in relation to a particular type of activity a single standard of care, this is arrived at only after consideration of subjective factors such as skill, knowledge, age or disability and the courts have accepted or rejected them as relevant on grounds of policy. As we have mentioned time and again the student who demonstrates his appreciation of the influence of policy considerations in the shaping of legal rules will undoubtedly impress an examiner. We hope that the following commentary on the relevant case law will assist the student in this respect and shed a little light on this confusing notion of a single standard.

Road Traffic Cases

In the context of personal injuries sustained in road traffic accidents, it would seem that the slightest momentary lapse of a driver of a motor vehicle may amount to negligence in law. Moral blameworthiness seems to have been divorced from legal responsibility. The point is well illustrated by the decision in *Roberts* v *Ramsbottom* [1980] 1 WLR 823. In this case, due to the restrictive attitude taken towards the defence of automatism, the defendant, who on the evidence had not completely lost control of his vehicle following a stroke, was held to be negligent. It is not without significance that the judge (pp. 829, 833) went out of his way to observe that no moral blame whatever attached to the defendant. In the earlier case of *Nettleship* v *Weston* [1971] 2 QB 692 the defendant, a learner-driver, was required, according to a majority of the Court of Appeal, to display the standard of skill of the ordinary, competent driver. These cases together appear to support the existence in law of a single, objectively assessed standard of care, a standard which subjugates moral blameworthiness to the notion of loss distribution, the latter being seen to be a major function of tort law, aided by the growth of liability insurance. Indeed, as far as drivers of motor vehicles are concerned such insurance is compulsory in respect of personal injuries to third parties, including passengers. The fact of such insurance ensures in this context that the notion of individual responsibility is replaced by that of collective responsibility, for it is the defendant's insurance company who will meet the bill for the plaintiff's injuries.

The decision of the Court of Appeal in this case, imposing as it does a single standard of care upon drivers of motor vehicles, would appear to have wider implications for the tort of negligence generally. Indeed, Megaw LJ in arguing in favour of a single standard stated (at p. 707):

> As I see it, if this doctrine of varying standards were to be accepted as part of the law on these facts, it could not logically be confined to the duty of care owed by learner-drivers. There is no reason in logic why it should not operate in a much wider sphere. The disadvantages of the resulting unpredictability, uncertainty and, indeed, impossibility of arriving at fair and consistent decisions outweigh the advantages. The certainty of a general standard is preferable to the vagaries of a fluctuating standard.

It is a fair question to ask whether and if so, to what extent, the principle of a single standard of care is more widely applicable? Let us look at some other areas to ascertain the position.

Medical Negligence

There appears to be a discernible difference in what might amount to a failure to exercise reasonable care here as opposed to cases in the previous category. As we have indicated, whilst the least momentary lapse of attention by a motorist might attract liability, the same cannot be said to be true in respect of injuries sustained during the course of medical treatment. We propose to explore the reasons why this might be so. However, before discussing that issue it should be recognised that the single objectively assessed standard of care referred to by Megaw LJ is somewhat misleading, for in this context subjective factors, namely the degree of skill and knowledge of the defendant, are taken into account (see *Bolam v Friern Hospital Management Committee* [1957] 1 WLR 582; contrast *Philips v William Whitely Ltd* [1938] 1 All ER 566). The appropriate standard is not that of the ordinary man in the street, but is as McNair J pointed out in *Bolam's* case (at p. 586): 'the standard of the ordinary skilled man exercising and professing to have that special skill'. The test is not completely objective because in the first instance it is necessary to discover whether the defendant has or professes to have the relevant skill or knowledge. Once it is found that he does possess that skill or knowledge, the test again becomes an objective one. Thus, in the words of Lord President Clyde in *Hunter v Hanley* 1955 SLT 213 at p. 217:

> In the realm of diagnosis and treatment there is ample scope for genuine difference of opinion and one man clearly is not negligent merely because his conclusion differs from that of other professional men, nor because he has displayed less skill or knowledge than others would have shown. The true test . . . is whether he has been proved to be guilty of such failure as no doctor of ordinary skill would be guilty of if acting with ordinary care.

The more recent case of *Luxmoore-May v Messenger May Baverstock* [1990] 1 WLR 1009 illustrates just how difficult the task of the plaintiff may be, particularly where the expert is being asked to give a valuation of property (paintings valued at £40, sold at auction for £840, subsequently resold at auction for £88,000; no negligence).

The distinction that we referred to above, between the way the law deals with victims of road traffic accidents and those injured in the course of medical treatment, stems not from the misleading notion of the single standard itself, but from the level at which the standard of care is set in the respective areas. Students should be aware of the decision of the Court of

Appeal in *Wilsher* v *Essex Area Health Authority* [1986] 3 All ER 801, wherein the court confirmed *that Bolam's* case requires the same standard of care to be shown by both trainee doctors and their more senior colleagues. The point was not raised on appeal to the House of Lords (see [1988] 2 WLR 557). That standard, it must be recognised, is substantially influenced by considerations of policy, which in this context, by way of contrast, operate against a finding of liability. The student should indicate what the relevant considerations are by perhaps discussing some of the leading cases. We have chosen two for this purpose, namely *Whitehouse* v *Jordan* [1981] 1 WLR 246 and *Roe* v *Minister of Health* [1954] 2 QB 66. In general terms it seems from these two cases that the courts are concerned to avoid creating a level of liability, which might, in their view, give rise to the phenomenon known as 'defensive medicine'. This practice has developed primarily in the United States as a result of the frequency and size of awards made against medical practitioners. It manifests itself in an over cautious approach to diagnosis and treatment which may result in a significant waste of time and resources. For example, a patient who complains of a headache may be subjected to a series of time consuming and complex tests to discover whether he or she is suffering from some serious medical problem. Students might point out that academics in general take the view that this fear of 'defensive medicine' on the part of the English judiciary may be exaggerated, bearing in mind the differences between the civil law systems in the United States and England. The courts' concern in respect of 'defensive medicine', and their concern to maintain the reputation of and confidence in the medical profession, have led to some difficulties in the articulation of the resulting 'lower' standard of care. The difference of opinion between the Court of Appeal and the House of Lords in *Whitehouse* v *Jordan* as to whether an 'error of judgment' amounted to negligence is perhaps the best illustration of this difficulty.

Sporting Activities

The decided cases concerned with injuries sustained by spectators at sporting events might also be used by the student to challenge the notion of a single standard of care. Whilst the number of cases is relatively small, they appear to give a clear indication that the standard of care demanded of a competitor, or indeed the organiser/occupier *vis-à-vis* the spectator is lower than that which may be demanded with regard to other activities. This results from account being taken of subjective factors in the determination of the standard of care. These personal factors relate not only to the defendant but also to the plaintiff. The student may recall that Lord Macmillan's dictum makes no mention of the 'personal idiosyncrasies' of the latter.

With regard to defendant competitors the courts have seen as highly relevant the fact that he or she is doing his or her best to win. A decision by the defendant 'in the agony of the moment' may amount to an 'error of judgment' rather than negligence (see, for example, *Wooldridge v Sumner* [1963] 2 QB 43). In this context also the courts have experienced difficulty in formulating satisfactorily this lower and subjectively influenced standard of care. This is clearly evidenced by the differing forms of expression used by members of the Court of Appeal in *Wooldridge v Sumner* and *Wilks v Cheltenham Homeguard Motor Cycle & Light Car Club* [1971] 1 WLR 668. In the former case Diplock LJ (at p. 68) suggested there would be no breach of duty 'unless the participant's conduct is such as to evince a *reckless disregard* of the spectator's safety' (emphasis added). In *Wilks*, whilst Lord Denning MR was prepared to adopt the 'reckless disregard of safety' test (at p. 670), Edmund Davies and Phillimore LJJ (at pp. 674, 676 respectively) took the view that the test was reasonable care in all the circumstances', including those mentioned above.

As we indicated earlier the courts in these cases have taken account of factors relating to the plaintiff, particularly that of consent. Whilst as a defence, consent (*volenti non fit injuria*) is rarely upheld by the courts, it may be taken into account, as here, as an element in determining the standard of care demanded of the defendant competitor. In the words of Sellers LJ in *Wooldridge* (at p. 56): '[P]rovided the competition or game is being performed within the rules . . . by a person of adequate skill and competence the spectator does not expect his safety to be regarded by the participant'.

The same consideration has to some extent influenced the standard of care demanded of an organiser of sporting events. As Lord Denning MR put it in *White v Blackmore* [1972] 2 QB 651 at p. 663, the spectator takes the risks inherent, for example, in motor racing which are unavoidable by the exercise of reasonable care. The student might usefully point out that this tells us very little unless we consider some of the cases which show what foreseeability and reasonable care have been taken to mean in this context (see *Hall v Brooklands Auto Racing Club* [1933] 1 KB 205 and *Murray v Harringay Arena Ltd* [1951] 2 KB 529). These cases would seem to indicate that the standard of care is set at a low level. Additionally, where the organiser has charitable status the courts may be reluctant to find against the defendant (see *White v Blackmore* per Roskill LJ at p. 674).

Other Situations

There exists a wide variety of situations in which the courts have been less than objective in establishing the appropriate standard of care. The decision in *Wells v Cooper* [1958] 2 QB 265 is one of the better known illustrations of this, where it was held that the standard of skill to be shown by a do-it-yourself enthusiast was not that of a skilled joiner or carpenter. Similarly, the age of the person whose conduct is in question, may well influence the standard of care. This is demonstrated by the cases in which contributory negligence has been alleged against child plaintiffs. The response of the courts has been to reject the argument that the same standard of care can be expected of a child as that expected of an adult (see *Gough* v *Thorne* [1966] 1 WLR 1387). Whilst there is a dearth of authorities as to the standard of care required of persons who are physically or mentally disabled, general academic opinion is to the effect that a court would be unlikely to impose on such persons the same standard expected of those not so disabled.

From the above discussion, a student should be able to conclude that the notion of the single standard of care only operates following an initial decision as to the relevance of subjective factors. Often that decision will be heavily influenced by policy considerations.

CONCLUSION

We would be the first to admit that there is a vast amount of material contained in the above discussion. Realistically, a student would be quite unable to use the whole of the material in the detailed way we have done. Selectivity and conciseness must be practised both before and inside the examination room. In the context of this particular question, the student should try to ensure that he or she makes some effort to include all three qualifications to Lord Macmillan's dictum. As we indicated in chapter 4 it might be perfectly acceptable to point out the various qualifications and concentrate your detailed discussion on one of them.

SELECTED READING

Atiyah, 'Res Ipsa Loquitur in England and Australia' (1972) 35 MLR 337.
Honore, 'Responsibility and Luck' (1988) 104 LQR 530.

6 NEGLIGENCE 3: CAUSATION AND REMOTENESS OF DAMAGE

INTRODUCTION

Of all the different aspects of negligence, causation and remoteness have, in our experience, proved to be the most difficult for students to understand well. This is hardly surprising in the light of Atiyah's comment in *Accidents, Compensation and the Law* (3rd ed., p. 122) that 'the technical or "conceptual" shape of this part of the law is a morass'. Assuming that there is a breach of the duty of care, the questions with which these two concepts are concerned are:

(a) Is the defendant's breach of duty in fact a cause of the plaintiff's harm?
(b) Is the defendant to be liable for all the harm which is linked to his breach of duty by a chain of factual causation, however tenuous?

The difficulties associated with these two questions may be highlighted, in a general sense, through the medium of two distinct types of case.

Illustration 1

Suppose a man presents himself during the night at the casualty department of a hospital complaining of stomach pains. After a cursory examination by a nurse, he is sent home with advice to see his general practitioner the following morning. He dies of arsenical poisoning later that day. These were substantially the facts of *Barnett* v *Chelsea & Kensington Hospital Management Committee* [1969] 1 QB 428 in which it was held that although there was a clear breach of duty on the part of the hospital staff, that breach of duty was not a cause in fact of the plaintiff's death. On the evidence accepted by the court, even if the deceased had been fully examined and treated properly, the probability was that he would have died anyway. This case illustrates how cause and proof thereof may be inextricably bound together.

Illustration 2

A employs B to cut down a tree in A's garden. Due to B's negligence the tree brings down the telephone wires into the roadway. C, a neighbour of A, realises the risk to traffic and rushes out to remove the wires. He has to leap out of the way of a car driven by D. In so doing he falls and aggravates an existing back injury. E, a mother with a baby in a pram, faints at the sight of the incident and the pram runs out of control down a hill. F, a bus driver, swerves to avoid the pram and collides with another vehicle, killing G, its driver. These are the facts of the case of *Salisbury* v *Woodland* [1970] 1 QB 324, with some embellishment. All the damage that results to the various parties can be factually traced to B's initial negligence. Is he to be held responsible in law for all the damage? Unless he is insured the imposition of full liability may be self-defeating, in that he may be unlikely to have the wherewithal to meet all the claims. If we were to require B to insure against such a potentially wide liability, what would be the cost of the premium? Whilst the policy of the law in limiting liability within what is perceived as manageable bounds is clear, the concepts and rules through which this is to be achieved are far from clear.

The issues of cause and remoteness may arise as part of a problem question or the sole topic of an essay. We propose later in this chapter to illustrate points of technique and explain the substantive difficulties using a problem-type question.

SUBSTANTIVE DIFFICULTIES

The structure we have adopted in this part is to look at the difficulties under three headings: causation in fact, remoteness, and problems of co-defendants and contributory negligence. We shall attempt, in so far as it is possible, to enable the student to see the wood for the trees. Our attempts to do this may be necessarily hampered by a significant degree of both conceptual and terminological confusion. For example, turning back to illustration 2 in the introduction to this chapter, different judges may deny G's ability to recover against B on the grounds either (a) that his injuries were not *caused* by B's negligence or (b) that G's injuries were too remote a consequence of B's negligence, namely, that they were not reasonably foreseeable. We can see that in the first of these approaches there is a selection process in operation. B's negligence is clearly a physical cause of G's injuries, namely he set in motion a chain of events which culminated in G's injuries. Yet a judge might well reject B's negligence as being a *cause in fact*. The selection process necessarily involves an assessment of the *causative potency* of a defendant's negligent act. As we shall see the two considerations which appear to be relevant to this assessment are the immediacy of cause and the degree of fault of the defendant. Inasmuch as the degree of fault is taken into account in this respect, this in turn will embrace the extent to which the resultant harm was foreseeable. However, the alternative approach through the notion of remoteness of damage also relies to a large extent upon the notion of foreseeability. The relevance of foreseeability to both approaches no doubt explains in part their interchangeability and the confusion which arises as a result. This position is not assisted by the distortion created by the influence of policy considerations to which we shall return later. The remainder of this section, as indicated earlier, we have structured in three parts, but the student should bear in mind the difficulties of the interrelationship between, particularly, causation and remoteness of damage which we have just discussed.

Causation in Fact

One of the first difficulties facing students is to understand what is meant by the so-called 'but-for' test which is conventionally employed in this connection. In particular, it is important that students should understand the limited function of this test.

Winfield on Torts (13th ed., p. 132) describes the test as no more than 'a preliminary filter', the purpose of which is to eliminate those breaches of duty which cannot in a physical sense be regarded as a cause of the plaintiff's damage. This limited function of the test can be seen by comparing the results it achieves in our earlier illustrations. In illustration 1, given that the court accepts the evidence of the defendant that the man would have died in any event, the result is that the defendant's negligence was not a physical cause of the patient's death. On the other hand, in the second of our illustrations, all the various items of damage sustained by the parties involved would pass through the 'preliminary filter' unhindered. Quite clearly a device of such crudity and limited effect is insufficient to confine liability within perceived policy limits. Not only is the test insufficiently selective in the relatively straightforward case, it is also inappropriate in the more complex cases involving 'consecutive' and 'concurrent' causes. There may also arise extremely difficult questions concerning the burden of proof. These matters are considered separately in the following paragraphs.

Consecutive and Concurrent Causes

The kinds of situation which give rise to special difficulty include those where the plaintiff is injured simultaneously by the negligent actions of two or more defendants. For example, A and B negligently shoot C at the same time. Each shot is sufficient to kill C, who in fact dies. It is clear that the 'but-for' test is of little value in such a case, as each of the defendants could point to the other as the cause of C's death. Fortunately, this type of incident rarely occurs in practice. What is much more likely (and is more likely to be found in examination questions) is the situation in which there may be two or more consecutive causes of the plaintiff's injury, as illustrated in cases such as *Baker* v *Willoughby* [1970] AC 467.

In view of the limitations of the 'but-for' test in cases of this kind, further refinement is necessary, which involves the courts in an evaluation of the causative potency of the conduct of the various defendants. This, it must be recognised, is a most unscientific process, because the notion of causation is being used to allocate responsibility in law. Responsibility tends to be imposed (i.e., causation established) the more immediate is the connection between the negligent act and the damage and the greater is the degree of perceived fault. The point was made forcefully by Lord Reid in *Stapley* v *Gypsum Mines Ltd* [1953] AC 663 at p. 681, that any logical scientific theory of causation is quite irrelevant in such situations. He went on to say that no hard and fast rule could be laid down by which to judge future cases. It was a matter of common sense in each particular case. His Lordship recognised that the task of attributing responsibility could be a most difficult one. It is also fair to say that it may be equally difficult from the student's point of view to try to predict in a hypothetical situation whether responsibility would or should be attributed to a particular defendant.

These difficulties are demonstrated by the well-known and troublesome cases of *Baker* v *Willoughby* (above) and *Jobling* v *Associated Dairies Ltd* [1982] AC 794. In *Baker* the plaintiff suffered injuries to his left leg as a result of the defendant's negligence. Prior to the date of trial the plaintiff was the victim of an armed robbery and sustained gunshot wounds in the same leg which necessitated amputation of the leg. The problem facing the court was the extent of the original tortfeasor's liability. Were damages to be assessed on the basis that the second incident had not occurred or did the occurrence of the shooting incident mean that the liability of the original tortfeasor was limited to the losses suffered prior to the date on which the leg was amputated? Had the House of Lords applied the established legal principles governing causation (i.e., the 'but-for' test) then the latter result would have been upheld. The departure from that principle by the House, based on vague notions of injustice, produced uncertainty in the law and no doubt some degree of consternation amongst law students. That consternation is certainly not removed by the later decision of the House in *Jobling*.

In this case the plaintiff suffered a disabling back injury as a result of the defendant's negligence. Before the trial, the plaintiff was discovered to be suffering from a pre-existing disease of the spine which was in no way connected with the accident but which rendered him totally unfit for work. In this case a unanimous House of Lords took a wholly different line. It was held that the illness had to be taken into account in calculating the defendant's liability, just as the possibility of post-trial illness would be taken into account in assessing damages for the loss of future earnings. The conflict between these two cases is further considered in the context of our commentary on the illustrative question later in this chapter. The conflict between these two cases themselves may not be the only source of difficulty for the student. The latter case clearly has implications with regard to the established rules concerning the assessment of damages and also the rule that the 'tortfeasor takes his victim as he finds him'. We would strongly advise students to consider very carefully the relationship between these various issues for, by so doing, a much greater level of understanding of the subject as a whole is likely to be attained.

A further but related problem which has troubled the courts on occasions concerns the question of whether the defendant's negligence has caused additional damage where the plaintiff or his property is suffering from some pre-existing defect (see *Cutler* v *Vauxball Motors Ltd* [1971] 1 QB 418; *Performance Cars Ltd* v *Abraham* [1962] 1 QB 33). The difficulty in this type of case lies in trying to decide whether or not the defendant has by his negligence exacerbated that pre-existing defect or conditions; see, for example, the differences of opinion in the Court of Appeal in *Cutler*.

Causation and the Burden of Proof

The issues of causation in fact and proof thereof are inextricably linked. This is illustrated by a number of recent cases, some of which are further complicated in that they raise again the issue of the relationship between causation and the rules governing the assessment of damages. The reaction of our students to these cases has been such that we believe students generally would welcome an uncluttered analysis which would enable them to gain a firm grasp of the more important basic principles.

Assuming that the plaintiff can establish that the defendant is in breach of a duty of care owed to him, the plaintiff is required to show on a balance of probabilities that the defendant's breach caused or made a material contribution to his damage. The plaintiff's case may well fall at this stage simply because he is unable to provide sufficient evidence that the defendant's breach was *capable of* causing his injury. This is illustrated by the decision in *Kay* v *Ayrshire and Arran Health Board* [1987] 2 All ER 417, HL, in which a young boy sought to recover damages for profound deafness allegedly caused by the clearly negligent administration of an enormous overdose of penicillin in the course of his treatment for meningitis. On the evidence, the House of Lords took the view that the probability was that the overdose was *incapable* of causing the child's deafness or even increasing the risk of such impairment (but see the critical note in [1988] SLT 25).

Even though the plaintiff is able to show that the breach is capable of causing the type of damage he has sustained, he still has the burden of showing that on a balance of probabilities the breach did cause or materially contribute to his damage.

Establishing the causal link between breach and damage is essentially a process of inference from the primary facts. The plaintiff must adduce sufficient evidence to enable a reasonable inference to be drawn that the breach caused or materially contributed to the damage sustained. 'It is not necessary, however, to prove that the [defendant's] negligence was the only cause of injury. A factor, by itself, may not be sufficient to cause injury but if, with other factors, it materially contributes to causing injury, it is clearly a cause of injury' (per Lord Salmon in *McGhee* v *National Coal Board* [1972] 3 All ER 1008 at 1017). We need only add that a 'material' contribution is one which is not negligible or *de minimis*.

There are inevitably cases in which the plaintiff has difficulty in discharging the burden of proof for want of, for example, sufficient medical evidence. The courts have on occasions shown a strong reluctance to allow a clearly negligent defendant to escape liability simply because of the plaintiff's difficulty in this regard. In *McGhee*, Lord Wilberforce took the view that 'where a person has, by breach of duty of care, created a risk, and injury occurs within that area of risk, the loss should be borne by him unless he shows that it had some other cause' (see [1972] 3 All ER 1008 at 1012). This proposed reversal of the burden of proof even in what may be termed 'marginal' cases has now been disapproved of by the House of Lords in *Wilsher* v *Essex Area Health Authority* [1988] 1 All ER 871.

Given that there exists considerable scope for the legitimate difference in the judicial view as to what inferences may reasonably be drawn from the plaintiff's evidence, students need to show an awareness that such views may well be influenced by value judgment and considerations of public policy. This is, we believe, readily apparent not only in the dictum of Lord Wilberforce (above), but also in the view expressed in the leading judgment of Lord Bridge in *Wilsher*, that 'we should do society nothing but disservice if we made the forensic process still more unpredictable and hazardous by distorting the law to accommodate the exigencies of what may seem hard cases' (see [1988] 1 All ER 871 at p. 883). The three cases recently heard in the House of Lords on the issue of causation, in which the plaintiffs' actions failed despite clearly established negligence, were all concerned with medical treatment (see *Kay* and *Wilsher* (above) and *Hotson* v *East Berkshire Health*

Authority [1987] 2 All ER 909 (below)). The result of these cases may be contrasted with that in a road traffic case, *Fitzgerald v Lane* [1987] 2 All ER 455, in which the Court of Appeal had to resolve a difficult point on causation, but did so in favour of the plaintiff with little inhibition. What is perhaps equally significant is that the issue of causation was not argued in the subsequent appeal to the House of Lords. Students might usefully consider whether the kind of policy distinctions we raised in chapter 5 in the context of breach of duty, are to some extent reflected here.

The fact that the decision in *McGhee* was recently considered in *Wilsher*, distinguished in *Hotson* but applied in *Fitzgerald*, will probably only serve to exacerbate the uncertainty surrounding *McGhee*. Students may recall that the majority in the House of Lords in the latter case rejected the argument for a reversal of the burden of proof and purported to apply their earlier decision in *Bonnington Castings Ltd v Wardlaw* [1956] AC 613. Their Lordships, however, went on to bridge the evidential gap by holding that the plaintiff had established that the breach had materially increased the risk of dermatitis and that was in effect the equivalent of showing that the breach had materially contributed to the injury and was sufficient to discharge the burden of proof.

The majority were determined to deny that there was any distinction between 'material increase in risk' and 'material contribution to the injury', or that any such distinction was relevant in the common law (see, for example, [1972] 3 All ER 1008, per Lords Reid, Simon at pp. 1011 and 1014 respectively).

Despite cogent argument to the contrary (see Weinrib (1975) 38 MLR 518) and the optimistic interpretation of most textbook writers, the House of Lords in *Wilsher*, whilst approving the decision in *McGhee*, has forcefully reiterated that the decision laid down no new principle (see especially [1988] 1 All ER 871 per Lord Bridge at p. 882). As a result of this cautious interpretation of *McGhee*, we are left with the proposition that, in *certain cases* it may be reasonable to infer that the breach was a material cause of the plaintiff's injury where the plaintiff can show that the breach substantially increased the risk of such injury but is, through force of circumstances, unable to establish more.

In which type of case might such an inference be drawn? The House of Lords in *Wilsher* refused to accept that such an inference could be drawn where the defendant's breach, even if it added to the existing risk of injury, was only one of six possible causes of that injury. In the light of this decision it may be that the *McGhee* approach is to be confined to situations where there is a particular risk, though emanating from different sources (including the defendant's breach; see cases such as *Bonnington* (above), *Bryce v Swan Hunter Group* [1988] 1 All ER 659, *Fitzgerald v Lane* (above)), as opposed to cases where there are several separate distinctive risks as in *Wilsher*. This distinction may prove too tenuous to sustain, for the signals are not yet clear enough to draw any firm conclusions. It may be that the policy considerations which we outlined above prove to be a more reliable guide. Students might like to consider the status of the decisions in *Bryce* and *Fitzgerald*, given that in both cases the court relied upon the extension of the *McGhee* approach adopted by Mustill LJ in the Court of Appeal in *Wilsher* [1987] QB 730 at pp. 771-2), which was subsequently reversed by the House of Lords.

The decision in *Hotson* (above) demonstrates an important distinction between the issue of causation and the question of the assessment of damages which students must fully understand. Where the court is concerned with the question of whether or not the defendant's breach caused the plaintiff's loss, then: 'in determining what did happen in the past a court decides on a balance of probabilities. Anything that is more probable than not it treats as certain', per Lord Diplock in *Mallett* v *McMonagle* [1970] AC 166 at 176. Assuming that a court reaches the conclusion that it is more likely than not that the breach caused the injury, the court does not then discount or reduce the plaintiff's damages 'by the extent to which he has failed to prove his case with 100 per cent certainty' (see *Hotson* (above) per Lord Ackner at 922). The decision in *Bagley* v *North Herts Health Authority* (1986) 136 NLJ 1014, in which such an approach was adopted, was expressly overruled in *Hotson*.

When, however, the court is concerned with the issue of assessment, damages may be discounted proportionately on the basis of future probabilities, i.e., that certain consequences may or may not follow from the proven injury. The stark contrast between the 'all or nothing' result on the issue of causation with that of the 'sliding scale' approach to assessment, is vividly illustrated by the decision in *Hotson*. In that case the defendants admitted negligence which caused delay in the diagnosis of the true nature of the plaintiff's injury. The defendants, however, denied that their negligence had caused the long-term disability which subsequently affected the plaintiff. At first instance Simon Brown J found that in the absence of negligence there was a 75 per cent chance that the long-term disability would have resulted. The learned judge went on to treat the problem as one of assessment (see [1985] 3 All ER 167 at 175) and accordingly awarded proportionate damages on the ground that the negligence had deprived the plaintiff of a 25 per cent chance of recovery. The decision was subsequently overturned in the House of Lords, where the issue was regarded as one of causation and their Lordships were unanimously of the view that the finding of fact by the judge that there was a 75 per cent chance that the long-term disability was caused by the initial accident meant that the plaintiff's action must fail in respect of this item of damage.

Students must take care as to the proper conclusions to be drawn from the decision. The House did not hold that there can never be liability for loss of chance of recovery in medical negligence cases. Indeed, their Lordships expressly left open the situation where the evidence of cause is inconclusive:

'Unless and until this House departs from the decision in *McGhee* your Lordships cannot affirm the proposition that in no circumstances can evidence of loss of a chance resulting from the breach of a duty of care found a successful claim in damages, although there was no suggestion that the House regarded such a chance as an asset in any sense', per Lord Mackay in *Hotson* (above) at p. 916.

In the light of the subsequent approval of the decision in *McGhee* by the House of Lords in *Wilsher*, the perceived injustice of the decision in *Hotson* in refusing to accept the 'deprivation of asset' argument may serve to encourage trial judges to 'discover' evidential gaps and to employ the *McGhee* approach to assist plaintiffs over the hurdle of proving cause.

Remoteness of Damage

We have already drawn the student's attention to the fact that the notions of causation in fact and remoteness are interrelated and to some extent interchangeable, or so it appears from the confused state of the case law. The following discussion will, however, proceed on the assumption that the plaintiff has established that the defendant's act was a cause in fact of his loss. The question now arises as to whether the defendant is liable for *all* of the plaintiff's losses. This can again be best expressed by looking at the facts of the leading case in this area, *The Wagon Mound (No. 1)* [1961] AC 388. Following a negligent spillage of oil from the defendant's ship the slipways on the plaintiff's wharf were contaminated with oil. Expert advice being given to the plaintiffs that the oil would not catch fire, the plaintiffs recommenced welding operations on the wharf. The oil ignited and the wharf was substantially damaged by fire. The Privy Council, in holding that the defendants were not liable for the damage by fire, rejected the former test for remoteness of damage (the 'directness test' as applied by the Court of Appeal in *Re Polemis* [1921] 3 KB 560). The Privy Council enunciated a new principle, namely, that the *type* of harm sustained by the plaintiff must itself be reasonably foreseeable. Whilst it must be acknowledged that the decision brought about a change in principle, subsequent case law would indicate little if any significant change in result. This state of affairs is a source of considerable confusion to students, in that they often fail to appreciate how there might be a significant change in principle without any corresponding change in result. Their difficulty is further compounded by the interrelationship between the *Wagon Mound* principle and the rules governing assessment of damages and the principle that the tortfeasor takes his victim as he finds him, a point made earlier in the context of causation in fact.

Assuming that the type of harm is foreseeable, students experience some further difficulty with two related issues. One is the extent to which the *manner* in which the harm is inflicted needs to be foreseeable. Distinctions drawn in some of the decided cases are not readily understood by students, see, for example, *Hughes* v *Lord Advocate* [1963] AC 837 and *Doughty* v *Turner Manufacturing Co. Ltd* [1964] 1 QB 518. This difficulty is equally true of the other related issue, namely, whether the *full extent* of the harm sustained by the plaintiff need be foreseeable, see, for example, *Vacwell Engineering Co. Ltd* v *BDH Chemicals Ltd* [1971] 1 QB 88.

We have made reference to the principle that the tortfeasor takes his victim as he finds him (the so-called 'eggshell skull' rule). Whilst it is well-established that this rule applies to personal injuries, it is not entirely clear whether it also applies to situations where damage is caused to property or where the loss is purely financial. Consequently, this is a point which examiners enjoy raising in examination questions.

Co-defendants, Supervening Events and Contributory Negligence

The need for this separate heading perhaps demonstrates the confusion which reigns in the case law on the issues of causation and remoteness of damage. Strictly speaking, it is our view that the matters discussed below ought to be regarded as issues of causation rather than remoteness of damage. However, the apparent interchangeability of the concepts of causation and remoteness, to which we have previously referred, as a means of attributing responsibility in certain cases has led us to afford separate treatment to these issues, in an attempt to dispel some of the uncertainty for the student.

The situations with which we are here concerned all involve the occurrence of some 'event' between the negligent act of the defendant and the plaintiffs suffering damage. A good deal of complexity arises in view of the different combinations of events which may occur. The following is an indication of the type of situations which quite often arise. The supervening event may be:

(a)   An act of human intervention, which itself may take the form of:

(i)   An act of a third party, which may or may not be tortious. If it is a tortious act, then the third party may be a co-defendant or himself the sole defendant. This situation may be illustrated by reference to *Knightly* v *Johns* [1982] 1 WLR 349 and *Clay* v *A. J. Crump & Sons Ltd* [1964] 1 QB 533. In the first of these cases, as a result of D1's negligence a one-way road tunnel was blocked. D2 (the police) subsequently took charge of the situation, but were negligent in discharging their duties, with the result that the plaintiff policeman was injured by D3. This occurred whilst the plaintiff was riding back against the flow of traffic in order to stop the traffic coming into the tunnel. The issue for the Court of Appeal was whether D1 bore any responsibility for the subsequent injuries of the plaintiff. Their conclusion was that he did not. The decision in *Reid* v *Sir Robert McAlpine Ltd* [1986] SLT

108 is a more recent and interesting illustration of this selection process, which resulted in the exoneration of one of the defendants. By way of contrast in *Clay* the plaintiff workman was injured when a wall on a building site collapsed. The building contractors (D1), the demolition contractors (D2) and the architect (D3) were held liable for a proportion of the damages.

The question has arisen in a number of relatively recent cases as to the extent of the responsibility, if any, of the person whose alleged negligence facilitates or fails to prevent an intentional tort by a third party which results in loss or damage to the plaintiff. Such liability is not of course without precedent (see *Home Office* v *Dorset Yacht Co. Ltd* [1970] AC 1004; *Stansbie* v *Troman* [1948] 2 KB 48). The more recent cases continue to show a marked reluctance to impose responsibility on the merely careless defendant in circumstances where the 'real' culprit is not discovered or not worth pursuing; see *Perl Ltd* v *Camden LBC* [1984] QB 342, *Meah* v *McCreamer (No. 2)* [1986] 1 All ER 943; contrast *Ward* v *Cannock Chase BC* [1986] 2 WLR 660, where on the special facts the plaintiff was at least partially successful. We would advise students to pay particular attention to the attempts to formulate an appropriate principle and to try to ensure that they are able to recognise the kinds of factors which are likely to determine decisions. In the latest cases the issue has been argued in terms of whether or not a duty of care might be owed to prevent torts being committed by others; see our advice in chapter 4 with regard to the decisions in *King* v *Liverpool City Council* [1986] 1 WLR 890, CA; *Smith* v *Littlewoods Organisation Ltd* [1987] 1 All ER 710, HL and *Topp* v *London Country Bus (South West) Ltd* [1993] 3 All ER 448, CA.

(ii)   The act of the plaintiff himself, which may or may not amount to contributory negligence, or which may result in the plaintiff being regarded as author of his own misfortune, thus denying him any remedy at all. Most recent and very interesting is the decision in *Cunningham* v *Reading FC Ltd*, *The Independent*, 20 March 1991, QBD, where the defendant football club was held liable for injuries caused to the plaintiff policeman by football hooligans.

(b)   A supervening natural event, which may add to the damage sustained by the plaintiff or which may be regarded as a new intervening cause (*novus actus interveniens*) which severs the link between the defendant's negligence and the plaintiff's loss.

Conclusion

In the foregoing pages we have drawn attention to the essential features of the topics of causation and remoteness of damage with which in our experience students find difficulty. In the light of what has been said in previous chapters on the issue of policy, the students should be aware that even at this late stage of the forensic process, such considerations may influence the court's view. Along with the apparently ever-present fear of indeterminate liability, the question of the availability and cost of insurance should not be overlooked, see, for example, *Lamb* v *Camden London Borough Council* [1981] QB 625.

ILLUSTRATIVE PROBLEM

Art is driving his lorry when, without warning, the brakes fail. He swerves in a desperate attempt to avoid Bart (a famous flautist earning £25,000 per annum). The lorry catches Bart a glancing blow before careering into a paint factory owned by Fargo. Chemicals leaking from the damaged vehicle mix with the paint causing an explosion which results in extensive damage to the value of £250,000 to the factory. Because of the ensuing fire hazard, the police evacuate Margot from her house next door.

Bart is taken to hospital suffering from cuts and a broken arm. He is given a tetanus injection by a nurse who, distracted by an emergency admission to the hospital and contrary to normal practice, fails to carry out a skin sensitivity test. Because of an unknown susceptibility, Bart reacts to the drug, becoming completely paralysed and suffering great pain. From the medical evidence it is uncertain whether he will recover. In the meantime thieves have entered Margot's house and stolen a number of valuable antiques worth £30,000. Discuss.

COMMENTARY

Introduction

The above problem clearly raises a large number of complex issues. Realistically, under examination conditions it would rarely be possible to include a detailed discussion on each and every one of those issues. Bearing this in mind it would seem sensible for the student to adopt a brief, concise style, with discussion of the facts of decided cases kept to a minimum. A number of the issues involved, however, demand to be treated in a more detailed fashion. The three issues in this problem, which, in our opinion, are deserving of such treatment are the question of the damage to the factory, the question of liability for theft of Margot's valuable antiques, and the question of the possible respective liabilities of Art and the hospital towards Bart. As we have indicated in previous chapters structure is all-important. Therefore, the advice previously given about the making of a rough plan should be followed. The potential plaintiffs are Bart (B), Margot (M) and Fargo (F) and the potential defendants are Art (A) and the hospital (H).

M v A

The liability of A to M could be argued in terms of the existence of a duty of care or in terms of causation/remoteness. The student may recall Lord Denning MR's statement in *Spartan Steel & Alloys Ltd* v *Martin & Co. (Contractors) Ltd* [1973] QB 27 to that effect and see, for example *P. Perl (Exporters) Ltd* v *Camden London Borough Council* [1984] QB 342. We propose to discuss it in terms of causation and remoteness as the Court of Appeal did in *Lamb* v *Camden London Borough Council* [1981] QB 625. Whilst the facts of the problem have been chosen to prompt a student in this direction, a student who analysed the issue in terms of duty or no duty would not be disadvantaged. (See *King* v *Liverpool City Council* (above), *Smith* v *Littlewoods Ltd* (above), to which we also referred in chapter 4.)

On the assumption that A does owe a duty of care to owners of property adjacent to the highway, he may well be in breach of that duty on the facts. It should be pointed out that the maxim *res ipsa loquitur* (the facts speak for themselves) may well be applicable in this situation, on the authority of the decision of the House of Lords in *Henderson* v *Henry E. Jenkins & Sons* [1970] AC 282. The student's attention is directed to this case by the examiner's choice of facts.

It being the case that A may be found negligent, it is clear that such negligence set in motion the chain of events which culminated in the theft of the valuable antiques. Thus the 'but-for' test may well be satisfied and resort must be had to the further stages in the selection process.

The likelihood is that M would be unable to recover the value of the antiques from A. As we indicated in the earlier part of the chapter, the process of reasoning by means of which this conclusion may be reached might differ as between judges. It is quite possible that a court could approach the matter in terms of causation, namely that A's breach of duty lacked sufficient causative potency to justify the imposition of legal responsibility. Indeed, this line of approach was employed by Lord Reid in *Home Office* v *Dorset Yacht Co. Ltd* [1970] AC 1004 at p. 1030, though the result in that case was that the defendant was held liable. Alternatively, a court might adopt the reasoning taken in *Lamb*, namely, that the damage was too remote. In that case the plaintiff's property had been damaged by squatters whilst unoccupied. It was unoccupied following the negligent bursting of a water main by the defendants which damaged the foundations of the property. The judgments are essentially couched in terms of remoteness, namely that the damage by the squatters was not a foreseeable consequence of the defendants' negligence.

Watkin LJ emphasised the wilful nature of the squatters' actions which he described as 'antisocial and criminal' (at p. 647). However, that of itself may not be sufficient to render such damage too remote (or sever the chain of causation). See, for example, the recent decision in *Cunningham* v *Reading FC Ltd* (above). The Court of Appeal in *Lamb* seemed to accept that the earlier decision in *Stansbie* v *Troman* [1948] 2 KB 48 was correct although Lord Denning MR had his doubts. In that case the theft from the plaintiff's premises was precisely the damage that the defendant painter and decorator was instructed to guard against. The resultant theft was therefore perceived as a *foreseen* consequence of the breach of duty. In *Lamb*, by way of contrast, the possibility of the damage by squatters was of a much lower order. The difficulty in this type of case lies in reliance upon an assessment of the likelihood and probability of the occurrence of such an event. A student may justifiably criticise expressions such as that used by Watkin LJ to the effect that a 'robust and sensible approach to the question of remoteness will often produce an instinctive feeling' that an event is too remote. Such 'instinctive' feelings are hardly a satisfactory substitute for principle.

It is implicit in the above discussion that the normal test of remoteness, namely, reasonable foresight of the type of harm, may be regarded as inappropriate in this category of case. In many cases the criminal activity of the third party would not be too remote and could lead to the imposition of too onerous a liability. This very point was made by Lord Denning MR in his judgment in *Lamb*, in which he also rejected the causation approach of Lord Reid in the *Dorset Yacht* case. Rather, he saw the issue being resolved through consideration of matters of policy, and in particular the availability of insurance (at p. 637):

> [T]he criminal acts here — malicious damage and theft — are usually covered by insurance. By this means the risk of loss is spread throughout the community. It does not fall too heavily on one pair of shoulders alone.

Where students choose to deal with the issue in terms of the existence or non-existence of a duty of care, they should be prepared to indicate the kind of factors which are likely to affect the outcome of any decision, some of which are fairly clear in the above-mentioned decisions in cases such as *Smith* v *Littlewoods Organisation* (above), *King* v *Liverpool CC* (above) and most recently *Topp* v *London Country Bus (South West) Ltd* (above).

The student ought to be willing to offer some comment upon the respective merits of the different justifications for the conclusion that A would not be liable to M.

F v A

The points already made on duty, breach and proof thereof with respect to any duty of care or breach of duty by A in our discussion of *M* v *A* are relevant here. One qualification might be that arguments concerning A's liability to F are more likely to be couched in terms of remoteness rather than terms of duty of care. It would, therefore, be sensible for the students to concentrate on these aspects.

The student should readily recognise that the 'but-for' test would be clearly satisfied on the facts and the point should be simply and briefly made. Furthermore, in view of the *immediacy* of the causal connection between the breach of duty and the impact with F's property, it is unlikely to be argued in terms of causation. There would seem to be little doubt that A would be liable for the impact damage to F's factory. The significant issue upon which argument should be focused is the extensive damage to the factory resulting from the explosion, and whether this is within the *Wagon Mound (No. 1)* principle. In dealing with this issue, a student would be well advised to give a clear statement of that principle, namely, that the *type of harm* sustained by the plaintiff must be reasonably foreseeable. It may be argued that the type of harm sustained both by impact and explosion is the same, namely physical damage to property. Such a broad view of the type of harm might be taken in the light of post *Wagon Mound* decisions, in particular, *Bradford* v *Robinson Rentals Ltd* [1967] 1 All ER 267. In that case the plaintiff's injury through frostbite, whilst unusual in the circumstances, was merely regarded as a particular form of a broader category of harm, namely, that which may result from exposure to extreme cold. In other words the particular form that the injury takes need not of itself be foreseeable, provided it falls within a more general category of injury which is foreseeable. The student might also refer by way of contrast to the case of *Tremain* v *Pike* [1969] 3 All ER 1303, where the category of foreseeable harm was narrowly construed.

It is arguable that a court, taking the view adopted in the latter case, might accept that damage to the factory by explosion was not in the same category as the impact damage. However, on the assumption that the opposite view was taken, further discussion should be addressed to the questions as to whether the harm needs to be foreseeable in the *manner* of its occurrence and/or its extent. On the authority of the decision of *Hughes* v *Lord Advocate* [1963] AC 837, the fact that a considerable part of the damage was caused by explosion rather than by impact may be regarded as immaterial. The House of Lords in that case held that harm which was of a foreseeable type was not too remote, even though it may occur in an unforeseeable manner. The decision is perhaps more easily understood as an illustration as to the meaning of foreseeability in negligence. As we pointed out in chapter 5, the test is based on what the courts deem to have been foreseeable with the benefit of hindsight, a point emphasised by Lord Wilberforce in *McLoughlin* v *O'Brian* [1983] 1 AC 410 at pp. 420-1. In *Hughes*, therefore, the fact that the child plaintiff was burnt not by naked flames but by an explosion brought about by the vaporisation of paraffin which had leaked from the lamp, would not be regarded by the reasonable man as unforeseeable. It must be emphasised, however, that even the hindsight of the reasonable man is subject to the qualification that a defendant should be only judged in the light of the state of knowledge at the time of the incident. It follows from this that the decision in *Hughes* is capable of being reconciled with the apparently conflicting decision in *Doughty* v *Turner Manufacturing Co. Ltd* [1964] 1 QB 518. It is apparent from the judgments in this case that, given the current state of knowledge, it was not foreseeable that an explosion could be caused by the immersion, whether accidental or deliberate, of the asbestos cover in a vat of hot, molten liquid. It would seem on the facts of the problem, that A's liability might turn upon whether, in the light of the current state of knowledge, the admixture of chemicals and paint would result in an explosion.

As to the issue of the extensive nature of the damage to the factory, if we assume that it is of a type which is held to be reasonably foreseeable, the fact that it is unforeseeable in its extent is not material, see, for example, *Vacwell Engineering Co. Ltd* v *BDH Chemicals Ltd* [1971] 1 QB 88. The student might usefully observe that the point reaffirmed in *Vacwell* is one example of a situation where, on this issue, there appears to be no difference between the principle in *Re Polemis* [1921] 3 KB 560 and the principle in *The Wagon Mound (No. 1)* [1961] AC 388.

B v A and H

This part of the problem is of considerable factual complexity and the student's difficulty will lie in satisfactorily structuring an answer in order to avoid confusion. It is an excellent illustration of a need for careful thought and for a little time to be invested in a rough plan. We suggest that the answer is started by looking at A's possible liability to B. We shall work first of all on the assumption that the hospital attracts no liability and then secondly, in the alternative, that it does. These alternative assumptions need to be made in order to provide a sensible structure for the discussion of the various issues. The basis for those assumptions needs to be discussed. The student will probably recognise that the facts of this question are designed to bring his or her attention to the decision of the Court of Appeal in *Robinson* v *Post Office* [1974] 1 WLR 1176. In that case the plaintiff had received a relatively minor injury at work as a result of the defendant's negligence. He was subsequently given an anti-tetanus injection at the hospital. He contracted encephalitis due to an allergy to the serum. We shall return to this case at a later stage. However, in this situation depending upon whether there is negligence on the part of the hospital, at least three different decisions are possible. The first is that the defendant might be held liable for the whole of damage, including the onset of encephalitis, the actions of the hospital not being regarded as a new intervening cause. Secondly, the defendants might only be liable for the slight injury, the actions of the hospital being regarded as an intervening cause and, indeed, the sole cause of the encephalitis. Any liability of the hospital would depend of course on proof of negligence on their part. Thirdly, in the event that no negligence was proved on the part of the hospital, it might be that nobody is responsible for the encephalitis. These respective liabilities may differ, in the light of the court's power to apportion damages as between them. On the facts in *Robinson* the Court of Appeal held that the hospital was not negligent and further that the Post Office was liable for all the damage suffered by the plaintiff. We shall return to the reasoning employed in that case in dealing with the first possibility.

B v A *(Hospital not Liable)*

As to whether A is in breach of a duty of care to B, it is permissible for the student to refer to the discussion on this question in the possible claim by M against A. Assuming A is in breach of a duty of care to B, is he liable for the full extent of the harm including that which follows the drug treatment? This would be the position if the reasoning in *Robinson v Post Office* [1974] 1 WLR 1176 was applied to these facts. This can be seen as an example of the 'eggshell skull' rule which is the line taken by Orr LJ (at pp. 1191-2):

> [I]f a wrongdoer ought reasonably to foresee that as a result of his wrongful act the victim may require medical treatment he is, subject to the principle of *novus actus interveniens,* liable for the consequences of the treatment applied although he could not reasonably foresee those consequences or that they could be serious.

The student can see here the effect of the use of the so-called 'eggshell skull' rule, in that it enables a plaintiff to recover as against the defendant for more extensive damage than that which was foreseeable. It is important that the student should notice that the defendants in *Robinson* owed a duty of care by virtue of the employer/employee relationship. The 'eggshell skull' rule is not being used here to create a duty, it merely goes to the extent of the harm, given that there is a duty. We shall refer to this issue again in chapter 8 on liability for shock.

B v A *(Hospital Liable)*

Assuming that for the purpose of discussion the hospital is to some extent liable (that issue on the facts will be dealt with below), the question to be considered here is the extent of A's liability. Negligence on the part of the hospital may well amount to a *novus actus interveniens* and thus as the sole cause of the paralysis and pain. In that event, A might only be liable for the minor injury and pain and suffering up to the time of the injection. However, the decision of the House of Lords in *Baker v Willoughby* [1970] AC 467 would seem to suggest that A may be under extended liability in the sense that B's disability as a result of the broken arm is regarded as continuing beyond the time at which B received the injection. The student will recall that in *Baker* the plaintiff had sustained an injury to his leg as a result of the defendant's negligence. Subsequently, prior to the trial, the plaintiff was the victim of an armed robbery. He was shot in the same leg resulting in amputation. The defendant argued that his liability for damages extended only to the point in time of the second injury. The argument was rejected by the House on the basis that to allow that argument would result in manifest injustice to the plaintiff. The House of Lords held that the defendant was liable as if the second injury had never occurred. The difficulty with this is that it entails accepting the fiction that the plaintiff had not had his leg amputated and was still feeling pain, suffering and loss of amenity sustained in the original accident. The student would no doubt like a few words of explanation to elucidate the precise nature of the problem which arose in *Baker's* case. Let us begin by accepting that in those cases where successive torts each cause identifiably separate injury, no special difficulty arises in allocating the respective responsibilities of the tortfeasors and assessing the damages. However, difficulty does arise, as in *Baker* and perhaps on the facts of our problem also, where the injury caused by the first tortfeasor is subsumed within the further damage caused by the second tortfeasor. If the 'but-for' test was strictly applied to this type of situation the first tortfeasor would be in a position to argue that his or her liability ceased at the moment of the second injury. The second tortfeasor could argue that he or she is liable only for the additional injury, for example, in *Baker* the armed robber, had he been sued, would no doubt have argued that he was liable only for damaging and causing to be amputated a leg which was already seriously damaged. The manifest injustice perceived by the House of Lords lies in the possibility that the plaintiff whose damage is caused by two successive tortfeasors could be in a worse position than a plaintiff who suffers identical injuries at the hands of only one tortfeasor.

Whether the solution offered in *Baker* is good law is a difficult question in the light of the more recent decision in *Jobling v Associated Dairies Ltd* [1982] AC 794. We shall say more about this case below, but it is at least arguable that *Baker* is still good law with regard to the two successive torts situation such as the one illustrated by the facts of this problem.

B v A (Nobody Liable for the Paralysis)

Under this heading we are assuming that the hospital is not liable for the onset of the paralysis because the court makes a finding that there is no negligence by the hospital or its employees. We are also assuming that the court is not prepared to adopt the reasoning of the Court of Appeal in *Robinson v Post Office* [1974] 1 WLR 1176 and thus make A liable for the whole damage. Whilst this seems to be an unlikely line to be taken by a court, we feel that it does need consideration. The situation that then exists would be that the paralysis would be considered to have a non-tortious origin. The issue is then whether A's responsibility for the injuries to B's arm continues beyond the point in time of the onset of the paralysis, as in *Baker*, or whether the court would adopt the approach in *Jobling*. It may be recalled that, in the latter case, the onset of the plaintiff's disease which occurred after the initial tortious injury but before trial, was regarded as a 'vicissitude of life' which had to be taken into account.

The House reached this decision on the grounds that the possibility of the occurrence of such an event after trial is normally taken into account when assessing loss of future earnings. On the facts of our problem and with law as it presently stands, it is more likely that *Jobling* would be applied.

We must now turn to the issue of the possible liability of the hospital to B. If the court is not prepared to find negligence on the part of the hospital or its employees, then it is obvious that H is not liable. On the question as to whether H is negligent the facts raise one or two relevant points upon which the student might offer some comment. The first is the standard of care which is appropriate in cases concerning injuries sustained in the course of medical treatment. The second is the relevance of the fact that the customary practice is not followed and the third is the issue of the agony of the moment, namely, the emergency. We do not propose to discuss those here. The student is referred to the discussion of those matters in chapter 5. However, it is worth pointing out that in *Robinson* the failure to carry out a similar test was not regarded as negligence. The court went further and suggested that even if there was negligence, there was insufficient evidence to show a causal link between that negligence and the plaintiff's damage. Even if the test had been carried out, it would not have revealed the plaintiff's particular susceptibility.

If, on the other hand, the test would have revealed B's susceptibility to the injection, there would be no room to argue that the paralysis arose as a result of the earlier injury. The case is clearly distinguishable from those such as *Hotson* v *East Berkshire Health Authority* (above). Assuming on the facts of our problem that H is liable for B's paralysis, we need to consider the extent of its liability. H might well seek to argue that it should only be liable for causing harm to B, a person already injured and that damages should be assessed in the light of that. That proposition is implicit in the decision of *Baker* v *Willoughby*. This appears to be an application of the 'eggshell skull' rule to the disadvantage of the plaintiff and we are not altogether sure that such an approach would be taken, bearing in mind that most people arriving at hospitals are suffering already from injury or disease.

As a final point, in the event that either party is held liable to B, it should be pointed out that future loss of earnings is normally recoverable. The fact that their extent may be unforeseeable, namely B is a flautist earning £25,000 p.a., is immaterial. This is not an example of the 'eggshell skull' rule but is merely an established point within the *Wagon Mound* principle (see *Vacwell Engineering Co. Ltd* v *BDH Chemicals Ltd* [1971] 1 QB 88).

CONCLUSION

We are sure that students would agree that the illustrative question chosen raised some extremely difficult and complex points. It should be abundantly clear that students should have clarified their thoughts on the issues of causation and remoteness long before they get into the examination hall. In the examination itself the need for a structured plan before attempting to write an answer is amply demonstrated.

ILLUSTRATIVE QUESTION

Try this one when you have a quiet moment or two!

D owns a broken down building in a small rural village. He is hoping to obtain planning permission to demolish the building and erect two new houses on the plot. The building is used by gangs of youths to hold illegal drinking parties. Local residents have complained to D and called the police on numerous occasions to disperse these noisy and often violent meetings.

Despite these complaints the events continue and in 1994 a drunken youth sets fire to the building. The fire spreads to P's adjacent property, a Grade I listed building, causing damage estimated at 2 million pounds.

P is overcome by smoke and injures his leg whilst trying to rescue a small but valuable painting from the fire. Upon admission to hospital the precise nature of P's injuries is incorrectly diagnosed. P believes this delay is a cause of the permanent disability from which he now suffers.

Discuss the possible liability arising in negligence.

SELECTED READING

Boon, 'Causation and the Increase of Risk' (1988) 51 MLR 508.

Dias, 'Trouble on Oiled Waters; Problems of *The Wagon Mound (No. 2)*' [1967] CLJ 62.

Hill, 'A Lost Chance for Compensation' (1991) 54 MLR 511.

Jones, 'Paying for the Crimes of Others' (1984) 47 MLR 223.

Price, 'Causation — The Lord's Lost Chance' (1989) 38 ICLQR 735.

Rowe, 'The Demise of the Thin Skull Rule?' (1977) 40 MLR 377.

Stapleton, 'The Gist of Negligence, Part II' (1988) 104 LQR 389.

Weinrib, 'A Step Forward in Factual Causation' (1975) 38 MLR 518.

7 NEGLIGENCE 4: LIABILITY FOR DEFECTIVE PREMISES

INTRODUCTION

As we indicated in the preface of the third edition, the departure from the ratio of *Anns* v *Merton London Borough Council* [1978] AC 728 by the House of Lords in *Murphy* v *Brentwood District Council* [1990] 3 WLR 414, has led to some revision of both structure and content of the book.

The effect of the decision in *Murphy*, together with the earlier decision in *D & F Estates Ltd* v *Church Commissioners for England* [1989] AC 177, is to remove from the law a substantial area of potential liability which might otherwise fall upon the shoulders of a range of persons and organisations who or which have in some way been involved in the construction of buildings, which subsequently prove to be defective. Local authorities, builders, surveyors and architects now owe no duty of care with regard to the remedial costs incurred by, e.g., a subsequent occupier. This is so despite the fact that the defective state of a building is a threat to the health or safety of the occupier and is the clear and obvious result of a failure to exercise reasonable care on the part of one or more of the aforementioned.

The liability which arose under *Anns* also posed some difficult questions on limitations. The Latent Damage Act 1986 was passed, at least in part, to ameliorate the savage restrictions placed upon the potential liability for latent damage by the House of Lords in *Pirelli General Cable Works Ltd* v *Oscar Faber & Partners* [1983] 2 AC 1. The later decision of the House of Lords in *Murphy* is particularly interesting in that their Lordships disregarded the fact that

Parliament, in passing the Latent Damage Act 1986, accepted *Anns* as good law. The decision in *Murphy* will, to some extent, reduce the importance of the 1986 Act.

In this revised chapter 7, we now consider not only the possible liability of the occupiers of defective premises arising out of the Occupiers' Liability Acts of 1957 and 1984, but also the residue of the potential liability of local authorities, builders, architects and surveyors following the decisions in *Murphy* and the *D & F Estate* case. It is our view that this residue may not be sufficient to justify any detailed consideration within the taught syllabus but may nevertheless provide at least a part of the subject matter of a problem question on defective premises. As a result of a little noticed change to the Defective Premises Act 1972, it may well be the case that whilst the decision in *Murphy* has closed one door another has been opened. In the light of that, we thought it might be useful to offer a view of the law following the decision in *Murphy*, although this is not raised as an issue in the illustrative question set out below.

SUBSTANTIVE DIFFICULTIES

The position after the decisions in *Murphy* and the *D & F Estates* cases.
In what circumstances, if any, might a local authority, builder, surveyor or architect, incur liability to, e.g., a subsequent owner/occupier of a building, rendered defective by reason of their negligence?

The answer to the underlying policy questions 'Who ought to bear such loss?' or 'Who ought to insure against such loss?' now appear to be the same whether the defendant is the builder or a local authority. Whilst not entirely settled, it seems reasonably clear that the broad principles of common law governing the classification of damage are now the same whether the defendant is a builder or a local authority. But in other respects there may be some significant differences between the potential liability of a local authority and that of a builder.

We need first to note that there are at present two potential sources of liability, the Defective Premises Act 1972 and the common law.

Liability Under the Defective Premises Act 1972

It is of the first importance to recognise that the statutory duty created by s. 1 of the 1972 Act in relation to new construction work applies only to dwellings and not to other buildings. The scope of that duty is further and severely restricted by s. 2 of the Act which has hitherto excluded dwellings covered by the NHBC Vendor/Purchaser Insurance Scheme. Since most building societies and banks are unlikely to lend on new properties not covered by that scheme the vast majority of new properties erected in recent years will have been within that scheme and persons involved in the construction of new dwellings will not generally have been subject to this statutory duty of care.

However, as pointed out by Duncan Wallace in (1991) 107 Law Quarterly Review 228, '*Anns* Beyond Repair', at p. 242, a fundamental and little noticed change in the above-mentioned position has taken place. At some date before 1988, the s. 2 exemption was 'effectively revoked' with the result that the fact that the dwelling was built under the NHBC Scheme no longer bars an action under s. 1 of the Act. Under this section an action may be brought against a wide range of possible defendants including not only builders, surveyors and architects, but also local authorities (see s. 1(4)(b) of the Defective Premises Act 1972).

The claim by Duncan Wallace (ibid, at p. 243) that '*Murphy's* abolition of *Anns*' liability, coupled with this latest and startling development, renders the 1972 Act of paramount importance to prospective plaintiffs', is in no way an exaggeration.

The action for breach of statutory duty under s. 1 of the 1972 Act differs in certain respects from an action at common law. Perhaps the most important of which is that the cause of action under s. 1 is deemed to arise at the time the dwelling is completed. The limitations period applicable by virtue of the Limitation Act 1980 expires six years from that date even though the defect in the dwelling could not have been discovered within that period. By comparison claims under the common law in respect of latent defects benefit from the extended limitations periods introduced by the Latent Damage Act 1986. Section 1 of this Act gives to subsequent purchasers a three-year limitations period which does not begin to run unless and until the damage was 'discoverable', subject to an absolute long stop of 15 years.

Liability Under the Common Law

The decisions in *Murphy* and the *D & F Estates* case have effectively removed the possibility of a successful tort action by the occupier of premises in respect of the remedial costs which result from the negligence of local authorities or builders. This is so even though the defects in the building present an immediate threat to the health and safety of the occupier. This conclusion flows from the insistence of the House of Lords in both cases that such loss is to be categorised as 'economic loss' as opposed to property damage and as such is not recoverable under the principle in *Donoghue* v *Stevenson* [1932] AC 562. The potential liability which survives these decisions may be considered under the following heads.

Personal injuries
There are clear dicta in both *Dutton* v *Bognor Urban District Council* [1972] 1 QB 373 and in *Anns* v *Merton London Borough Council* [1978] AC 728, to the effect that the immunity previously enjoyed by the negligent builder of a

defective building under the common law no longer exists. Such a person would now be liable under the *Donoghue* principle. Whilst the House of Lords in *Murphy* has overruled the first case and refused to follow the decision in the second case, it seems reasonably clear from the judgment of Lord Bridge in *D & F Estates v The Church Commissioners for England* [1988] 3 WLR 368, at p. 376, that the House of Lords did not seek to gainsay that dicta, at least in regard to builders.

By way of contrast, although the point did not fall to be considered on the facts of *Murphy*, there are indications in a number of the judgments that a local authority may not owe a duty of care even in respect of personal injury. To date there have been no cases in which the negligence of a local authority has led to the sudden collapse of a building and consequent personal injury, though the prospect of such an event is certainly not beyond reasonable contemplation. In the light of that one may legitimately point to the fact that the Public Health Act 1936 and the Building Act 1984 under which the powers of control are conferred upon local authorities are concerned with health and safety.

Property damage or economic loss?
It comes as no surprise that the courts have had difficulty in drawing a readily ascertainable dividing line between what is to be regarded as economic loss and what is property damage. Yet the consequences which flow from this less than precise categorisation are fundamental.

Where the negligently inflicted loss is regarded as purely economic, it is recoverable only in very limited circumstances. Such loss is recoverable under the principle of detrimental reliance established in *Hedley Byrne v Heller and Partners* [1964] AC 465. Economic loss is also arguably recoverable in other circumstances where there exists a close proximate relationship between the parties even where there is no detrimental reliance by the plaintiff on the defendant, see cases such as *Ross v Caunters* [1980] Ch 297; *Ministry of Housing and Local Government v Sharp* [1970] QB 223; *White v Jones* (1995) *The Times*, 17 February. Whether the decision in *Junior Books Ltd v Veitchi Co. Ltd* [1983] 1 AC 520, falls into this latter category is debateable.

In practical terms, despite the fact that the harm caused to subsequent occupiers by the negligence of either local authorities or builders is readily foreseeable, the proximity which exists between the prospective litigants will not normally be such as to permit recovery of what is now regarded as economic loss namely, the cost of remedying the defects in the building itself.

The complex structure theory
This theory, advanced by Lord Bridge in *D & F Estates v The Church Commissioners* [1988] 3 WLR 368, at p. 386, was considered in a number of the judgments in *Murphy*, with little enthusiasm. In essence the theory maintains that, in the context of complex structure, where one part of a structure is

defective and causes damage to another part of the structure, that damage could be classed as damage to property rather than economic loss. Where such damage resulted from negligence, liability might follow under the broad *Donoghue* v *Stevenson* principle. This may be so even though the whole of the structure had been conveyed as a single entity to e.g., the plaintiff occupier.

We suspect that the prospects of success of this argument are likely to be variable. In regard to local authorities the argument is likely to have little if any success at all. Whereas in *Anns* itself, the negligence of the defendant council led to the construction of defective foundations, we cannot imagine that a court would be prepared to regard the resultant damage to the upper structure as damage to 'other' property. This would amount to an almost total evasion of the decision in *Murphy*.

Similarly, where a single builder has constructed the different parts of the structure and one defective part damages another the argument is unlikely to meet with success. The position may be different where the defective part is clearly distinguishable from the part damaged and the two parts were constructed by different persons. A simple example would be where defective wiring was installed by a subcontractor in a new building and which led to the destruction of the whole building which had been completed by a main contractor/builder. As Duncan Wallace points out in (1991) 107 LQR 228, at p. 239, many difficult and arbitrary cases may well arise. Such issues may well be raised and discussed in the context of your seminar discussions and could find favour with your examiner.

THE LIABILITY OF THE OCCUPIER OF DEFECTIVE PREMISES

In the second part of this chapter we are concerned with the possible liability under the Occupiers' Liability Acts 1957 and 1984, which may be incurred by those persons who retain a sufficient degree of control over premises.

A clear distinction in law exists between the duty of an occupier of premises towards lawful visitors on the one hand and trespassers on the other.

With regard to the duty owed to lawful visitors, there are few difficulties of a conceptual nature for the student. Such conceptual difficulties as exist in the law arise mainly in the context of the duty (if any) which is owed to trespassers. Whilst the difficulties in this area are not of the same order as those in the previous chapter, this is nonetheless a popular examination topic which a student seriously ought to consider including in his or her revision programme.

SUBSTANTIVE DIFFICULTIES

(a)   The initial difficulty facing the student in this area is to decide who is an occupier for the purposes of both the 1957 and 1984 Acts. The answer will not be found in either Act, for both refer to the common law test (see s. 1(2) of the 1957 Act and s. 1(2) of the 1984 Act). The fact that the answer has to be divined from the case law and the fact that the test, namely the sufficient degree of control test, embraces the possibility of more than one occupier of premises, causes students some difficulty. The situation where in law there is more than one occupier, each having a different area of control, serves to increase that difficulty. For example, the facts in *Wheat v E. Lacon & Co. Ltd* [1966] AC 552 are a good illustration of this point. The premises were a public house and it was recognised that both the licensee and the brewery were joint occupiers with quite different areas of control. The degree of control test which was reaffirmed in *Wheat v E. Lacon & Co. Ltd* permits the possibility than an independent contractor working upon premises may be classed as an occupier of some part of those premises. The fact that there may be more than one occupier of the whole or part of the premises was expressly acknowledged by Lord Goff in the recent decision of the House of Lords in *Ferguson v Welsh* [1987] 1 WLR 1553 at p. 1564. His Lordship made a further interesting observation to the effect that a person may be a lawful visitor *vis-à-vis* one of the occupiers but not so with regard to another occupier of the same premises.

(b) One extremely important issue is the distinction which is drawn between lawful visitors and trespassers. The central aim of the 1957 Act was to dispose of the highly artificial distinctions as between different classes of lawful visitor which existed at common law. However, the distinction between lawful visitors and trespassers remains a matter of common law, the dividing line continuing to be drawn very often by reference to the doctrine of implied licence which may be difficult to apply in practice. In our experience students do not demonstrate a sufficient appreciation of the historical perspective which needs to be taken of the doctrine of implied licence in this context. Prior to the decision in *British Railways Board v Herrington* [1972] AC 877 the courts resorted to the doctrine with some degree of readiness, at least in cases where children were injured by dangerous allurements, in order to avoid the harshness of the law as laid down by the House of Lords in *Robert Addie & Sons (Collieries) Ltd v Dumbreck* [1929] AC 358. Given the higher standard of care required of occupiers *vis-à-vis* trespassers following the decision in *Herrington* and the 1984 Act, the courts will no longer find it necessary to employ the fiction of implied licence in order to find in favour of the injured plaintiff.

An occupier remains free to place restrictions upon a visitor in terms of the parts of the premises he may lawfully visit, the purposes for which he is permitted to enter premises, or the duration of his visit. A person who enters premises as a lawful visitor may therefore become a trespasser in the event that he exceeds those limits. This matter is again dealt with by the common law and not by either of the Occupiers' Liability Acts. The case law supports the view that reasonably clear notice of any such restrictions must be given to a lawful visitor if his non-observance of those restrictions is to render him a trespasser. What amounts to sufficient notice will no doubt depend upon the facts of any particular case. An examiner may well choose to create such a situation in an examination question to prompt a student to argue the issue both ways, i.e., according to whether the plaintiff was a lawful visitor or a trespasser at the time he sustained injury. The examiner may also take this opportunity to test the student's understanding as to the relevance, if any, of notices such as 'Private, Keep Out', and as to the defences of *volenti* or contributory negligence which the occupier may raise.

(c) The 1957 Act lays down that a common duty of care is owed to all lawful visitors, thus ridding the law of the problem of the variation in standard of care required with regard to invitees and licensees under the common law. However, the Act expressly acknowledges that the standard of care demanded of an occupier may be higher with regard to children than that in relation to an adult.

Just how far an occupier must go to satisfy the standard of care was discussed in *Morgan* v *Blunden* (1986) *The Times* 1 February. The Court of Appeal held that the duty of an occupier of an unsupervised adventure playground did not extend to requiring a system of inspectors to ensure that nothing happened to render the premises unsafe. The court held that it was not reasonably foreseeable that a third party might leave an abandoned vehicle with smouldering rubbish against it which exploded, injuring the plaintiffs.

Furthermore, recognition is given to the point that visiting tradesmen are substantially responsible for their own safety, at least as regards risks which are necessarily incidental to their particular trade or calling. Despite the fact that these points are spelt out clearly in the Act, students quite often fail to deal with them adequately or at all when they are raised in examination questions.

(d) An issue which an examiner might frequently exploit is the extent to which an occupier is liable, if at all, where a lawful visitor is injured as a result of the negligence of an independent contractor employed by the occupier. Again, despite the fact that the matter is dealt with specifically in the Act, students confuse this issue with the quite separate issue as to the possible liability of the contractor himself *as* occupier. There was some discussion of the possible liability of an occupier for the earlier omissions of an independent contractor in *Ferguson* v *Welsh* (above). In particular Lord Keith of Kinkel (at p. 1560) made some observations on the liability of an occupier for an unsafe system of work adopted by an independent contractor.

(e) Perhaps the most attractive aspect from the examiner's point of view is the possibility that the occupier's liability to a lawful visitor may be affected by an exclusion clause. It is one of a small number of situations (contract apart), in which liability in negligence may be affected in this way. It therefore presents the opportunity for the examiner to test the knowledge and understanding of the restrictions upon the use of exclusion clauses which apply in this context by virtue of the Occupiers' Liability Act 1957 and the Unfair Contract Terms Act 1977. The limits of, and the distinctions within, the controls created by the above-mentioned Acts are not in our experience dealt with particularly well by the average student in examinations.

(f) The relationship between occupier and visitor also gives rise to the possibility that the occupier may discharge his duty of care by giving to visitors an adequate warning of hazards which exist upon the premises. This principle is expressly recognised, in somewhat cautious language, by s. 4 of the 1957 Act and s. 1(5) of the 1984 Act. An examiner may well seek to elicit from students a clear explanation as to the relationship between that provision and the defences of *volenti* and contributory negligence which may also be avaiable to an occupier.

(g) Two recent cases have highlighted some interesting points on the extent of an occupier's duty. In *Ogwo v Taylor* [1987] 3 WLR 1145 the Court of Appeal held that an occupier who negligently set fire to his premises owed a duty to a professional fireman who was injured as a result of fighting the fire. It was not open to the occupier to argue that this was within the risk of a fireman's occupation; the appropriate test was reasonable foresight in accordance with *The Wagon Mound (No. 1)* [1961] AC 388. The Court of Appeal stressed that no distinction was to be made between 'ordinary' and 'exceptional' risks.

In the other case, *Smith v Littlewoods Organisation Ltd* [1987] 1 All ER 710 (see also *King v Liverpool City Council* [1986] 3 All ER 544), the House of Lords commented on the liability of an occupier of premises towards occupiers of adjoining property. In that case the House held that the respondents were under a general duty to exercise reasonable care to ensure that the condition of their premises, which were awaiting demolition, was not a source of danger to adjacent property. Whether there was a specific duty to prevent damage by fire brought about by vandals on the respondents' premises depended on whether it was reasonably foreseeable that, if no action was taken to keep the premises secure, they would be set on fire with consequent risk to neighbouring properties. On the facts given, that the respondents had not been aware of the vandalism in the area, the events were not reasonably foreseeable (see *Sedleigh-Denfield v O'Callaghan* [1940] AC 880). A topical issue arose in the very recent case of *Cunningham v Reading Football Club Ltd, The Independent*, 20 March 1991. The issue facing the High Court was whether the football club was liable to a police officer on duty at the ground who was struck by a lump of concrete thrown by a member of the crowd. The judge held them liable as occupiers because the club knew that there was an unruly, violent element amongst the visiting crowd and the concrete was in such a state that it could easily be broken off in lumps. This had occurred on another occasion a few months before. A prudent occupier would have taken steps to minimise the risk. It might be asked how this case fits in, if at all, with the cases discussed in chapter 5 (see, e.g., *King* v *Liverpool City Council* (above)).

(h) With regard to an occupier's liability towards a trespasser, as indicated above, the issue is now covered not by the common law, but by the Occupiers' Liability Act 1984 with effect from 13 May 1984. Students are likely to find difficulty with the interpretation and application of the provisions of this Act to any given fact situation for at least three reasons. First, of necessity the rules embodied in the Act are of a broader, open-textured nature. This can be seen from the only reported decision so far on the Act, *White* v *St. Albans City and District Council* (1990) *The Times,* 12 March. Secondly, the provisions of the Act themselves are not particularly well-drafted and appear to be ambiguous on some important points. Thirdly, the student needs to appreciate that liability *vis-à-vis* trespassers has to be decided by interpreting these provisions, and not normally by reference to the common law decisions in *British Railways Board* v *Herrington* and subsequent cases. There is a general tendency amongst lawyers to relate back to the common law and the student needs to understand the circumstances and the extent to which this is permissible. The Law Commission in their Report on Liability for Damage or Injury to Trespassers (1976, Cmnd 6428) took the view that all the decided cases after *Herrington* were correct in result. As a consequence the temptation to relate back to them may be all the stronger.

(i)   The first major issue under the 1984 Act is when does the duty of care arise? In particular the question of the degree of knowledge which the occupier is required to have both of the risk itself and the presence of the trespasser before the statutory duty of care arises: see *White* v *St. Albans City and District Council* (above). Students often fail to appreciate that the statutory duty is not owed to *all* trespassers. By way of contrast to the situation of the lawful visitor, the mere presence of the trespasser does not automatically give rise to a duty of care under the Act. An interesting question is precisely what duty is owed to trespassers who are not within the scope of the 1984 Act?

(j)   As we have pointed out the duty of care is formulated in broad terms, as is the standard of care owed to trespassers who are within that duty. The difficulty for the student may well be in the fact that a number of considerations are relevant to both the duty and breach issues. Unlike the 1957 Act, the broadly worded provisions of the 1984 Act do not identify the factors which assist in establishing the appropriate standard of care in any given fact situation. Again, there may be a temptation to go back to the earlier cases. Questions which the student might consider are: Is the test as to the occupier's knowledge an objective or subjective one? Are the occupier's resources to be taken into account? Is there a difference of approach on the issue of standard of care as between child and adult trespassers? Is the nature and purpose of the trespasser's entry onto the land relevant, for example, the burglar who is injured whilst on the premises?

(k) A final issue in connection with trespassers, again a matter not covered by the 1984 Act, relates to cases of injury to trespassers by persons who are not occupiers of the premises. For example, a child trespasses on X's land and climbs a tree and is electrocuted by high-voltage cables hidden in the foliage of the tree. The cables are owned by D. Assuming that there was negligence on the part of D, of what relevance to a claim against D is the fact that the plaintiff child was a trespasser on X's land? These are broadly speaking the facts of *Buckland* v *Guildford Gas Light & Coke Co.* (1949) 1 KB 410, where the court found for the child. Dicta in *Herrington's* case (Lords Wilberforce and Pearson [1972] AC 877 at pp. 914 and 929 respectively) may cast some doubt on this decision, but the position is even more uncertain in view of the fact, as mentioned, that the liability of non-occupiers is not covered by the 1984 Act.

ILLUSTRATIVE QUESTION

Percy took his small son, Sidney, to a fair owned and operated by D. Entry to the fair is free. The fair was held on land owned by L, a local farmer. Though L permitted this use once each year he always erected a notice, prominently displayed at the entrance to the fair, which excluded all liability on his part for 'any injury, loss or damage howsoever caused, whether arising by reason of negligence or otherwise'.

At the fair Percy left Sidney at a side-show while he searched for a toilet. Unable to find one Percy unbolted and went through a gate in the fence surrounding the fair on to other land owned by L. While seeking a quiet spot he fell through some rotten boards covering an old well-shaft and was seriously injured.

Sidney, an inquisitive child, had in the meanwhile pushed his hand through a very small hole in a guard on an electric generator, badly injuring his hand.

Discuss.

COMMENTARY

The comments made in previous chapters as to the wisdom of making a rough plan before writing an answer are equally applicable here. Indeed, a few moments' reflection on this problem should enable a student to see clearly how the answer can be sensibly structured, and that the first issue to be dealt with is that of the possibility that there are two occupiers, each having their separate area of responsibility under the 1957 and 1984 Acts. Thus we can see there are two potential defendants (D and L), and also two potential plaintiffs, Percy (P) and Sidney (S).

From the facts of the problem both D and L would be regarded as occupiers under the legislation. There can be little doubt that L is the occupier and he has not relinquished control over that part of the land where the disused well is situated. The well is clearly within his area of responsibility as the sole occupier. As for D it would appear that the generator is on part of the land over which he has a sufficient degree of control, the test laid down by Lord Denning in *Wheat* v *E. Lacon & Co. Ltd* [1966] AC 552 at p. 577. The decision in *Fischer* v *CHT Ltd (No. 2)* [1966] 2 QB 475 may be used to support the argument that a person whose control over premises is of a very temporary nature may nevertheless have a sufficient degree of control and thus be an occupier. In the event that it was held that D did not have a sufficient degree of control over the land upon which the fair was positioned, it is certainly possible to argue that he had exclusive control over the generator itself. Such equipment could arguably, strangely enough, be 'premises' as defined in s. 1(3) of the 1957 Act. Even if he could not be regarded as an occupier as discussed above, he may nonetheless be liable at common law. The fact that any liability arising may be by virtue of the common law as opposed to under the Act, is unlikely to be of any significance on the facts of this particular case.

We suggest that the question of the structure of the answer has now been resolved, into a claim by S against D and one by P against L.

S v D

The first issue to resolve here is whether S is to be regarded as a lawful visitor and this is a matter regulated by the common law. Because entry to the fair is free, the claim will be in tort, not contract. There is no doubt that when P and S enter the fairground they are both lawful visitors to whom the common duty of care is owed by virtue of s. 2(1) of the Occupiers' Liability Act 1957, subject to the exclusion clause, the effectiveness of which is discussed below. The important question which arises as regards S is whether he remains a lawful visitor, once his father leaves him unattended. The age of S is deliberately left vague, he is merely described as a small son. That the occupier's liability to children may vary has been recognised in the decided cases. If, for example, S was 15 years of age, there is little doubt that he would continue to be regarded as a lawful visitor. However, if he is a very young child, some of the earlier cases suggest that, if unaccompanied, the child would be treated as a trespasser. This approach, sometimes awkwardly referred to as the 'conditional implied licence' was considered by Devlin J in *Phipps* v *Rochester Corporation* [1955] 1 QB 450 at p. 470 as unsatisfactory in view of considerable difficulties in its application, although it appears to have received the approval of the Court of Appeal in *Bates* v *Stone Parish Council* [1954] 1 WLR 1249. Devlin J preferred to regard young children as implied licensees, and thus lawful visitors, but thought that in deciding whether the occupier had discharged the duty of care (then owed under the common law) the behaviour of the parents in allowing the child to be on the premises unaccompanied should be taken into account. In this respect occupiers are entitled to assume that a reasonably prudent parent would not allow the child to visit premises unaccompanied without satisfying themselves that the premises were safe. There may be occasions when it would be imprudent to let a child go on to premises without being accompanied by an adult.

There seem to be two issues here. The first is whether the presence of the child, unaccompanied, was reasonably foreseeable by an occupier. Secondly, given that the child's presence is foreseeable, what standard of precautions is required? Turning to the facts surrounding S's injury, it might be forcefully argued that as the premises in question are a fairground, S's presence, unaccompanied, may be reasonably foreseeable. It must be borne in mind that S arrived accompanied and it is quite common for children of all ages to become separated from the most prudent of parents (see, for example, on this point the decision of *Moloney* v *Lambeth London Borough Council* (1966) 64 LGR 440) given that S's presence is foreseeable. The standard of care required of an occupier is higher in respect of children, according to s. 2(3)(a) of the 1957 Act. However, in a recent case *Simkiss* v *Rhondda Borough Council* (1983) 81 LGR 460 (CA), it was held that the standard required of the occupier in this respect was no higher than that of the prudent parent. On the facts in our problem, this issue can be argued either way. On the assumption that P had acted prudently, it would seem clear from the decision in *Moloney* that the occupier may be liable even though the source of danger which caused the injury to the child would not have been a source of danger to an adult. The fact that the hole in the guard of the generator may have been too small for an adult's hand to pass through would not appear to be of any assistance to the occupier. In *Moloney* a child was playing on a stairway in a block of flats which was under the control of the defendants. The child fell through a gap in the balustrade through which an adult could not have fallen. The defendants were held liable.

In the absence of any evidence that D had taken any steps to warn children off or fence off the generator which itself might be an allurement to children, on balance we would suggest S would be regarded as a lawful visitor and that D would be in breach of his duty of care towards him.

In the event D sought to rely on the notice containing the exclusion clause, displayed at the entrance to the fair, two or three points may be raised. Its effectiveness in principle may depend on the age of the child, in that S may be below the age at which he might reasonably be expected to understand the meaning of such a notice. Further, it is not certain whether D can rely on the notice as it was placed there by L. Even if these two points can be satisfied, as D is a business occupier within the meaning of s. 1(3)(b) (as amended) of the Unfair Contract Terms Act 1977, s. 2(1) of the Act will prevent reliance on the clause in so far as it purports to exclude liability for death or personal injuries.

As a concluding point in S's claim against D, the student might consider mentioning that, depending on S's age, D might seek to raise the defence of contributory negligence. Although there appears to be no fixed age below which a child cannot, in law, be guilty of contributory negligence, it is accepted that the standard of care expected of a child for its own safety is lower than that which is expected of an adult (see *Gough* v *Thorne* [1966] 1 WLR 1387).

P v *L*

In our earlier discussion we suggested that L alone would be regarded as the occupier of the area in which the disused well is situated.

The central and most difficult issue raised in this part of the question is whether P, at the time he was injured was a lawful visitor or a trespasser. Whilst it is necessary to discuss the cases which may help to resolve this issue, in all probability a student would be unable to say conclusively whether P fell into one or the other category. It would, therefore, be advisable to discuss L's liability to P first of all on the assumption P might remain a lawful visitor and, secondly, on the assumption he becomes a trespasser when he goes through the gate in the fence on to the adjoining land.

The student may well be aware of a number of cases which touch on this issue. Perhaps the decision which would give most support to the argument that P remained a lawful visitor is that of the Court of Appeal in *Pearson* v *Coleman Bros* [1948] 2 KB 359. Indeed the facts of the problem have been chosen to prompt the student to this case. It will be recalled that the defendants, circus owners, were held liable for injuries sustained by a seven-year-old girl when she strayed from the circus to the zoo part of the premises in search of a toilet. Lord Greene MR (at p. 375) stated:

> A person who has two pieces of land and invites the public to come to one of them can, of course, if he chooses, limit the invitation to that one; but if the other piece is contiguous to that one and he does not indicate to his invitees that his invitation is confined to the one piece of land, he cannot be surprised if they treat his invitation as extending to both pieces. In my opinion, if a land owner is minded to make part of his land a prohibited area he must indicate this to his invitees by appropriate means.

Lord Greene went on to say that the 'rough and ready' method of marking the zoo off from the circus might have been sufficient on the facts to indicate to an adult that the zoo was a prohibited area, but not sufficient with regard to the child plaintiff. However, the Court of Appeal in *Pearson* did approve of its earlier decision in (*Gould* v *McAuliffe* [1941] 2 All ER 527. In this case the plaintiff was treated as an invitee in respect of that part of a public house where she mistakenly thought that there was a toilet. To reach this part of the premises she passed through a gate which was open at the time. Scott LJ took the view that the plaintiff acted reasonably in what she did, pointing out that the gate was not locked nor was there any notice on it indicating that the yard was private.

Whilst *Pearson* was concerned with a child plaintiff, it was not a case on allurement, in which licence has in the past been more readily implied in favour of children. Consequently, it may not be possible, despite Lord Greene's view expressed above, for L to argue that *Pearson* is distinguishable on the facts of our problem on the basis that P is an adult. L, as we know, owns both pieces of land and it is by his invitation that the public comes on to the fairground. Therefore, in these circumstances it is a question of whether he has taken sufficient steps to indicate that going beyond the fence is prohibited. Whilst (unlike *Gould* v *McAuliffe*) the gate is bolted, there is no notice which indicates clearly that entry on to the adjoining land is not permitted, bearing in mind that he has good reason to believe that there will be considerable numbers of people attracted to the fair. On the facts P may be regarded as having acted reasonably and, therefore, be treated as a lawful visitor.

If that is the position, the question arises as to whether L is in breach of the common duty of care owed under s. 2(1) of the 1957 Act. Whilst the question does not demand a detailed discussion on this issue, the student might point out that the standard of care on the occupier involves taking reasonable care to see that the visitor is reasonably safe for the purposes for which he is invited or permitted by the occupier to be there (s. 2(2) of the 1957 Act). A student might usefully indicate the kind of factors which might be relevant in deciding whether L has exercised reasonable care. These might include his knowledge of the existence of the well, the seriousness of the danger, the likelihood of the presence of people and the duration of the state of disrepair.

Assuming breach could be established L might turn to the exclusion clause in the notice displayed at the fairground entrance. Whether he would be able to rely on that clause depends on whether or not L is a business occupier of the part of the premises beyond the fairground. The facts of the problem indicate that the land in question is farmland and that would seem to fall within the definition of 'business' in s. 14 of the Unfair Contract Terms Act 1977, thus attracting the provision in s. 2(1) which prevents the exclusion of liability for personal injuries resulting from L's negligence. The fact that a visitor's purpose is in no way connected with the occupier's business is normally irrelevant. However, the position is somewhat complicated by an amendment to s. 1(3) of the Unfair Contract Terms Act 1977 by s. 2 of the Occupiers' Liability Act 1984. The upshot of that amendment would appear to be that a business occupier who allows part of his premises to be used for the purposes of an educational or recreational visit is now permitted to exclude liability to such visitors. This amendment does not apply where the provision of educational or recreational facilities is a business purpose of the occupier. It would seem from the facts of the problem that L, a farmer, may well be able to take advantage of the amendment in the circumstances. The exclusion clause contained in the notice displayed at the entrance to the premises would therefore not be subject to s. 2(1) of the Unfair Contract Terms Act. The clause may, however, need to satisfy the requirements of the common law, which appear to survive with regard to notices of this type aimed at non-contractual visitors. In *Ashdown* v *Samuel Williams & Sons Ltd* [1957] 1 QB 409, it was decided that the common law rules applicable in contract law generally are applicable in this context also. Thus, provided that reasonably sufficient notice of the clause has been given, and provided also that the terms of the clause adequately cover the liability which would otherwise have arisen the clause will be effective. Both these requirements appear, on the facts, to be satisfied. The clause is prominently displayed at the entrance and expressly excludes liability for negligence in terms. However, criticisms were levelled at the approach taken in *Ashdown*. In particular Lord Denning MR in *White* v *Blackmore* [1972] 2 QB 651, at pp. 665-6 expressed concern to the effect that the ability to exclude the liability seriously undermines the purpose of the provision in s. 2(4)(a) of the 1957 Act, which clearly encourages occupiers to warn lawful visitors of dangers. Why bother warning educational or recreational visitors, when it is just as easy, if not easier, simply to exclude liability by an adequately worded and prominently displayed notice, as in our problem? The students might question whether this is a satisfactory situation, given that visitors of this kind, frequently children, will be less appreciative of dangers or risks on what are after all business premises.

Let us now consider the possible liability of L to P, on the assumption that P is a trespasser at the time of his injury. Since the position is now governed by the 1984 Act the previous common law decisions such as those in *British Railways Board* v *Herrington* [1972] AC 877, *Southern Portland Cement Ltd* v *Cooper* [1974] AC 623, *Pannett* v *P. McGuinness & Co. Ltd* [1972] 2 QB 599, *Penny* v *Northampton Borough Council* (1974) 72 LGR 733, are of no authority as to the proper interpretation of the provisions of the 1984 Act, though reference to those decisions is permissible to discover the purpose of the Act. As mentioned before the only decision of any value in this context is *White* v *St. Albans City and District Council* (above). One of the factors considered in that case was the fencing off of the land, but in addition, the issue of whether the field was used as a short cut on a regular basis by people trying to reach a car park was also relevant. This may be pertinent to (b) below. Students may well be unclear as to what is expected of them and how they should deal with this aspect of P's claim against L. We would suggest that the student should demonstrate to the examiner that he appreciates the present difficulties, which are likely to continue for some time given the relative paucity of actions of this kind. Beyond that an examiner would expect the student to explain the major points of contention which arose in the earlier common law decisions (in so far as they are relevant to the briefly stated facts in the problem itself) and to indicate the difficulties (if any) of resolving those points under the Act.

The most sensible approach would be to begin by stating the relevant provisions of the Act. In doing so it should be emphasised that the statutory duty is not owed to all trespassers but only to those who can satisfy the requirements of s. 1(3). In this respect P will have to establish that:

(a)　L is aware of the danger or has reasonable grounds to believe it exists; and

(b)　L knows or has reasonable grounds to believe that P is in the vicinity of the danger concerned or that he may come into the vicinity of the danger, whether or not P has lawful authority for being in that vicinity or not; and

(c)　the risk is one against which in all the circumstances of the case, L may be reasonably expected to offer the other some protection.

Perhaps the difficult issue here is the degree of knowledge on the part of L which P needs to show before the duty is owed. The provision in (a) above would seem to clarify the pre-existing law in the sense that actual knowledge of the danger need not be proved. On the facts of our problem if it can be proved L has knowledge of the danger, namely the existence of the well and the state of disrepair of the boards this would clearly satisfy point (a). This may be difficult to establish, but nonetheless P may succeed on this point if he can show L had reasonable grounds to believe that the danger existed. In the absence of proof of actual knowledge as to the primary facts, the question arises as to what would amount to reasonable grounds for belief, given the apparently subjective nature of the language and the absence of any further information in the problem.

In the light of the fact that L has given permission for part of his land to be used as a fairground, it should not be too difficult to show that L had reasonable grounds to believe that P might come into the vicinity of the danger, thus satisfying point (b). Additionally, given the seriousness of the danger represented by the disused well, it may well be that this is a risk against which he may reasonably be expected to offer P some protection, within point (c).

Assuming on the facts that P establishes that L owes him the duty of care within the provisions of s. 1(3) of the 1984 Act, P must then show that L was in breach of that duty. As we indicated in the earlier part of this chapter, there would seem to be some confusion in the sense that a number of consider-ations are relevant to both the existence of that duty and the breach of that duty. We have already come across this type of difficulty in chapter 5 when discussing breach of duty of care in general terms. The student will recall that we pointed out that foreseeability of injury to the plaintiff is relevant both to the issue of duty in fact and also to the breach of that duty. As we went on to say, breach is essentially concerned with measuring the quality of the defendant's conduct in the light of a certain degree of probability of risk of harm to the particular plaintiff and to that extent it involves the consideration of a number of factors such as cost, social utility and so on. That two-stage process of analysis is reflected in this Act. Thus, whilst the extent of the occupier's knowledge as to the presence of the trespasser and the danger concerned is relevant to the issue of breach, subsections (4) and (5) of s. 1, will in addition involve the consideration of a number of other factors in deciding whether L has taken such care as is reasonable in all the circumstances. It is not clear whether the occupier's resources are to be taken into account in deciding whether sufficient care has been taken. Even if the provision is to be interpreted in this subjective fashion, on the facts the cost of repairing or maintaining the boards would hardly be onerous to L. One further point is that one of the factors which may well be taken into account is the purpose of the trespasser. It seems reasonably clear that there will be a significant distinction drawn between the standard owed, for example, to a burglar, and that owed in respect of a relatively innocent trespass such as that of P. Should liability against L be established in the light of the previous discussion, the final issue is whether or not as against a trespasser L can rely on the exclusion clause. There is considerable academic debate as to whether this is possible. There are at least three feasible ways of approaching this issue. First, 'reasonable care' as required by s. 1(4) of the 1984 Act may be regarded as amounting to a 'negligence' liability for the purposes of the Unfair Contract Terms Act 1977, in which case L, being a business occupier, cannot rely on the exclusion clause in so far as it relates to P's personal injuries by reason of s. 2(1) of the 1977 Act. Whether the amendment to s. 1(3) of the 1977 Act, discussed earlier, would apply so as to prevent L being regarded as a business occupier is not clear. Secondly, it could be argued that 'reasonable care' *vis-à-vis* a trespasser is of a lower standard than is owed generally in the tort of negligence and does not qualify as negligence within s. 1(1) of the 1977 Act. In that event, provided L's clause satisfies the common law tests, discussed earlier, then it will provide a defence. Thirdly, it is possible to argue that the standard of care imposed under the statutory duty in the 1984 Act represents an irreducible minimum and cannot therefore be excluded even by a clause satisfying the common law controls.

CONCLUSION

On one or two issues, the student will appreciate that, notwithstanding, or perhaps because of, statutory intervention in this area there are significant difficulties. Those illustrated in the problem above will serve to demonstrate the importance for the student to have clarified his thinking on this area long before examination time.

ILLUSTRATIVE QUESTION

Here is one which we thought of earlier!

Dave owns a warehouse, the ground floor and yard of which is let to Risky Ltd for use as storage space for crated goods prior to export. The crates are stacked on pallets and fork lift trucks are used to store and remove the crates from the warehouse. At the main entrance to the warehouse there is a notice which states 'Warning — Industrial Premises, the management accepts no responsibility for injury, loss or damage suffered by anyone using these premises'.

The yard is surrounded by a low wall which is, on occasions, scaled by teenagers taking a short cut across the yard to a nearby bowling alley.

Hans, one of Risky Ltd's trade customers, visits the warehouse and is injured when a number of crates which are stacked near the front gate fall on his car as he enters the yard.

Mike, 15 and his brother Peter, 13, climb the wall on their way to the bowling alley. Mike climbs on a fork lift truck and, finding the key in the ignition starts the engine. He loses control and breaks his leg when the fork lift truck runs out of control into the warehouse wall. Peter runs for help and is injured when he falls from the wall because some of the bricks are loose. Peter's jacket and trousers are bloodstained and his watch and spectacles are broken.

Discuss the possible liability in tort to Hans, Mike and Peter.

SELECTED READING

Clark, 'Occupier's Liability After the Unfair Contract Terms Act 1977' (1981) 10 Anglo-American LR 1.

Grubb, 'A Case for Recognising Economic Loss in Defective Building Cases' [1984] CLJ 111.

Law Commission: Report on Liability for Damage or Injury to Trespassers 1976, Cmnd 6428.

Mesher, 'Occupiers, Trespassers and the Unfair Contract Terms Act 1977' [1979] Conv (NS) 58.

Spencer, 'The Defective Premises Act 1972: Defective Law and Defective Law Reform' [1974] CLJ 307.

Wallace, 'Anns' Beyond Repair' (1991) 107 LQR 228.

8   NEGLIGENCE 5: PERSONAL INJURY SUSTAINED THROUGH SHOCK

INTRODUCTION

Where a person intentionally and directly inflicts personal injuries upon another, whether mental or physical, it matters not that the injury so caused resulted from impact or shock (sec chapter 3 and particularly *Wilkinson* v *Downton* [1897] 2 QB 57). Where, however, personal injuries result from the *negligent* conduct of the defendant, the position is quite different. There exists a well-established distinction in the extent to which plaintiffs may recover for personal injury sustained through shock rather than impact. The existence of this distinction in law and its effect, together with the question of its justification, are matters of practical significance and of considerable interest to academics. Not surprisingly the issue is likely to be included in most tort syllabuses and appears with some frequency in examination papers.

In our discussion of the duty of care in negligence in chapter 4 we pointed out that personal injury sustained through the negligent infliction of shock, was not actionable simply on the grounds that it was foreseeable, as is largely the case where personal injury is a result of negligent impact. Concern as to the possibility of fraudulent claims, the uncertainty of medical prognosis and the fear of creating 'indeterminate' liability, gave rise to the judicial view that the public interest would be better served by restricting recovery for injury by shock. This led to the imposition of certain severe and arbitrary limits being placed upon the foreseeability principle in such cases.

With the evolution of a more enlightened social policy, supported and indeed promoted, by some members of the judiciary, a number of those restrictions have now been discarded, some have been eased, whilst others remain. Some of the conceptual difficulties may have been to some extent glossed over by approaching the issue of restriction in terms of the prima facie duty as enunciated by Lord Wilberforce in *Anns* v *Merton London Borough Council* [1978] AC 728. This is no longer the case. As we pointed out in chapter 4, the approach to the duty issue presently preferred is that any expansion in the law should be by way of cautious increment, rather than being driven by broad principle.

The issue of the extent to which 'nervous shock' is actionable may be examined in a full question which may be either a problem or an essay question. Alternatively some aspect of the topic may appear as one amongst a number of issues in a more widely drawn problem question. We would suggest therefore that if, as is more than likely, the topic is included in your syllabus, you would be wise not to neglect revision of it. In chapter 2 we emphasised how important it is that students should make every effort to resolve any difficulties of substance or technique long before examination time. In this context we would draw the student's attention to two specific matters.

The first is a need for constant and independent research to keep abreast of the developments in the law. Important cases have an awkward habit of being reported close to examination time, after lectures and seminars have ceased. An examiner could not fail to be impressed by a student who is able to include discussion of such cases in an examination script.

Secondly, in *McLoughlin* v *O'Brian* [1983] 1 AC 410, at least one member of the House of Lords supported the view expressed by the Court of Appeal that the whole issue would be better dealt with by legislation. Furthermore reference is made in the judgments of Lords Wilberforce, Scarman and Bridge, and more recently in the House of Lords in *Alcock* v *Chief Constable of South Yorkshire* [1991] 4 All ER 907, to the existence of legislation in New South Wales and the Australian Capital Territory dealing with the issue of nervous shock. As a part of the normal process of formulating a view on substantive issues, students should consider the desirability and possible effect upon the present common law of the enactment of similar legislation in the United Kingdom. Sensible and accurate observations on this matter in an examination script would undoubtedly impress the examiner.

SUBSTANTIVE DIFFICULTIES

Students will normally experience little difficulty in recognising a question or part thereof as being concerned with nervous shock. The subject does, however, involve a number of quite difficult and interrelated substantive points which are likely to exercise the student's mind more than a little. At this stage we shall merely identify the substantive difficulties. We shall, as in previous chapters, expand upon those difficulties in the commentary on the illustrative question.

Students need to be clear in their own minds what is meant by this rather misleading term 'nervous shock'. We are here concerned with situations in which harm to the plaintiff has been inflicted by means of shock rather than by impact. But it is also true that the harm actually sustained by the plaintiff in all the cases has been of a psychiatric rather than a physical nature. Perhaps the first question to be addressed is what constitutes actionable harm in such cases. Does the restricted duty of care, to which we refer below, extend to emotional disturbances such as grief and sorrow?

This chapter is essentially concerned with those cases in which psychical harm has been caused by 'a sudden attack on the senses', resulting from the occurrence of some traumatic event often on a large scale e.g., the sinking of the ferry *Herald of Free Enterprise*, the fire at King's Cross underground station, the Hillsborough tragedy and, most recently, the Piper Alpha disaster.

We would wish to avoid giving the impression that these cases preclude from action other harm of an emotional nature, sustained in other circumstances. The categorisation of harm as 'nervous shock' is not only misleading but may well inhibit the development of the common law. Students must appreciate that what constitutes actionable harm in a broader sense and the circumstances in which a duty might be owed in that regard, are the subject of constant debate and litigation. A student's understanding of these broader issues might well be tested by a suitably aimed question in the light of the recent decisions in *Taylor* v *Somerset Area Health Authority* (1993) 4 MLR 34 (QB), *M* v *London Borough of Newham, P (Minors)* v *Bedfordshire County Council* and also *Khorasandjian* v *Bush* (above, chapter 3).

Assuming that a plaintiff has suffered legally recognised harm through shock, what degree of proximity needs to be established between plaintiff and defendant to give rise to a duty of care in law? The point was made with some force in chapter 4, that in numerous situations the mere foreseeability of the harm sustained by the plaintiff may not be sufficient to place the defendant under a legal duty to avoid causing such harm. This is certainly true where the injury is of a psychiatric nature resulting from shock rather than impact. In such cases there is a clear policy of recognising only a restricted duty of care. The cases reveal a number of specific restrictions which operate upon the foreseeability principle. These restrictions are most relevant in those cases of fear for the safety of others, or the sight of injury to others (whether at the scene of the accident or by witnessing the aftermath).

The uncertainty which continues to cause difficulties in these cases lies not so much in being able to identify those restrictions, for they are openly articulated in the cases themselves. Rather, the difficulty lies in being able to predict what restriction, or combination of restrictions, will be regarded as both necessary and sufficient to keep liability within boundaries which are acceptable to the judiciary. The main purpose of these restrictions is then to avoid the imposition of indeterminate liability upon the defendant. But what is 'indeterminate liability'? Is it the amount which the defendant may fairly and reasonably be asked to pay, commensurate with the degree of fault on his part? Alternatively, is the notion of indeterminate liability coloured not so much by the degree of fault on the part of the defendant but rather by some vague judicial impression of the possible impact upon the size of liability insurance premiums?

The uncertainty in the law arising out of the divisions of opinion in *McLoughlin* v *O'Brian* (above) has been addressed. The House of Lords in *Alcock* v *The Chief Constable of South Yorkshire* [1992] 1 AC 310 preferred the more structured and more restrictive approach of Lord Wilberforce in *McLoughlin* to the more flexible and liberal approach to be found in the judgments of Lords Bridge and Scarman. First instance decisions in which this latter approach was utilised to find in favour of plaintiffs have been either reversed on appeal (see *Ravenscroft* v *Rederiaktiebolaget Transatlantic Ltd* [1992] 2 All ER 407n, CA) or disapproved of in *Alcock* (*Hevican* v *Ruane* [1991] 3 All ER 65).

Despite the adoption of the more restrictive approach of Lord Wilberforce in *McLoughlin* by the House of Lords in *Alcock*, the unanimity of the conclusions reached in *Alcock* is unfortunately not matched by a unanimity of reasoning. A further feature of the judgments is that they avoid laying down strict limits, anticipating any further developments on a case by case basis. The various judgments have been praised on the one hand for their pragmatism, yet criticised as being 'disappointingly vague' on the other.

There is therefore some likelihood of continuing division in judicial opinion as to where the boundary on liability is to be drawn. The recent cases indicate an extremely cautious line being taken (see, e.g., *Taylor* v *Somerset Health Authority* [1993] 4 Med LR 34; *McFarlane* v *EE Caledonian Ltd* [1994] 1 All ER 1, CA; *Taylorson* v *Shieldness Produce Ltd* (1994, CA, unreported, LEXIS)).

What are the Restrictions?

We are here concerned with cases where the plaintiff suffers psychological injury as a result of fear for the safety of another person (V), or the sight of injury to another person (V). In order to establish a duty of care in such cases, it is necessary but not sufficient that psychological harm is foreseeable. In addition, the following restrictions apply:

(a)   Generally there must be some close relationship of love and affection between the plaintiff (P) who suffers shock and the person whose safety is threatened or who is the victim of the accident (V). On the facts of *McLoughlin* it was unnecessary to extend the law beyond those relationships recognised at the time, i.e., spouse and parents. Lord Wilberforce did accept the possibility that some less close tie might suffice though these 'must be judged in the light of other factors, such as proximity to the scene in time and place, and the nature of the accident' (*McLoughlin* v *O'Brian* [1983] 1 AC 410 at p. 422).

This statement graphically highlights the point we made above, namely that the existence of a duty is determined by a combination of factors. The combination which is regarded as both necessary and sufficient may be difficult to predict.

In *Alcock*, in addition to recognising certain specific exceptions to this 'relationship rule' such as rescuers (*Chadwick* v *British Railways Board* [1967] 1 WLR 912) or those plaintiffs who are 'unwilling participants' in the event (*Dooley* v *Cammell Laird Ltd* [1951] 1 Lloyd's Rep 271), the possibility of a duty being owed to a stranger was accepted. But in what circumstances such a duty might arise is far from clear. How close to the event would a stranger need to be? How horrendous must the event be? Lord Ackner's tanker example in *Alcock* ([1991] 4 All ER 907 at p. 919) may be thought to give some indication of the answers to these questions, but see *McFarlane* v *EE Caledonian Ltd* (above).

There exists some uncertainty and controversy with regard to the quality of the 'ties of love and affection'. The very idea of the existence of a duty of care depending upon the proof of such matters is arguably repugnant and yet the House of Lords has indorsed this requirement and indeed used it as a ground for dismissing a number of the appeals with which they were concerned.

The matter is to be dealt with on an evidential basis by way of rebuttable presumption which operates in favour of spouses and parents but against other familial relationships. We therefore face the uncertain prospect of cases being decided on the basis of some pretty unsavoury arguments.

(b)   Even assuming that the relationship between P and V is one of love and affection, there are further restrictions which must be met. The decision in *Hambrook* v *Stokes* [1925] 1 KB 141, approved in *McLoughlin* restricts the duty of care to those who experience shock through their 'own unaided sense'. Lord Wilberforce in *McLoughlin* envisaged that this might be satisfied by a person seeing on live television, an accident (or the immediate aftermath) involving a close relative.

In *Alcock*, all the claims based on communication by live television were rejected either on the lack of relationship or on the grounds that the live television coverage of the event could not, on the facts, be 'equiparated with the viewer being within sight or hearing of the event or its immediate aftermath' per Lord Keith, [1991] 4 All ER 907 at p. 915.

Yet again, the conclusion reached by their Lordships was unanimous but the reasoning appears to be almost in total disarray. A similar disparity in reasoning can be seen in the views of the Court of Appeal in *Jones* v *Wright* [1991] 3 All ER 88, where the court reversed the decision of Hidden J on this point. Despite having rejected all claims on the facts, the possibility of such a claim succeeding is not completely ruled out in *Alcock* (see especially Lord Ackner [1994] 4 All ER 907 at p. 921).

One certain result of the application of the 'own unaided senses' rule, is the exclusion from any duty of care of persons, including parents and spouses, who suffer shock upon hearing the news of tragic events involving their loved ones, via a third party. It is perhaps beyond question that injury through shock to parents and spouses in particular is highly foreseeable in these circumstances, and yet the House of Lords in both *McLoughlin* and *Alcock* has not been prepared to recognise any duty of care towards them. As we pointed out earlier the decision to the contrary in *Ravenscroft* (above) has now been reversed on appeal and a similar decision in *Hevican* was expressly disapproved of in *Alcock*. Whilst the law on this point seems to be more certain, students will appreciate that it is regarded by many as unnecessarily restrictive and unjust and may well lead to some judicial acrobatics to avoid such results.

(c) The natural course of events following a tragic accident will often involve a visit to a hospital or a mortuary by the close relatives of the victim. In *McLoughlin*, the House of Lords accepted in principle that a duty of care could be owed at least to a close relative who sustains shock as a result of seeing the immediate aftermath rather than the accident itself.

> One who from close proximity comes very soon upon the scene (including the aftermath) shall not be excluded [per Lord Wilberforce [1982] 2 All ER 298 at p. 304].

Whether or not such proximity exists is essentially a question of fact and necessarily involves a degree of uncertainty. Whilst this factual uncertainty will inevitably lead to arbitrary decisions the problem is compounded. The absence of any consensus of reasoning in *Alcock* has left a legacy of additional uncertainty. What may or may not in law constitute the immediate aftermath is far from clear. Is the duty, for example, confined to those who are concerned to rescue or offer comfort? See the recent decisions in *Taylor* v *Somerset Health Authority* (above) and *Taylorson* v *Shieldness Produce Ltd* (above).

(d) The nature of the incident itself is another factor which deserves individual attention, although this is a matter which is often rationalised within the notion of foreseeability rather than being an additional limitation as are those considered above.

The courts have shown a willingness to differentiate between cases on the basis of the nature of the event which allegedly shocked the plaintiff. This can be seen in the early unsuccessful cases such as *Hay (or Bourhill)* v *Young* [1943] AC 92 in which Lord Porter at p. 117 expressed the view that:

The driver of a car even though careless is entitled to assume that the ordinary frequenter of the streets has sufficient fortitude to endure such incidents as may from time to time be expected to occur in them ... and is not considered negligent towards one who does not possess the customary phlegm.

What constitutes 'the customary phlegm' and whether or not an event is sufficient to foreseeably cause shock to a person of 'reasonable fortitude' is clearly a matter for judicial interpretation as can be seen from the more recent case-law, e.g., *McFarlane* v *EE Caledonian* (above).

What then of the plaintiff who is especially vulnerable to psychiatric injury? This of course raises the issue as to whether or not, in the nervous shock cases, the normal rule that the defendant takes his victim as he finds him, is displaced. Students need to appreciate that the issue raised here is one of duty rather than one of remoteness of damage, as it was in cases such as *Smith* v *Leech Brain and Co.* [1962] 2 QB 405. The more recent cases seem to suggest a less lenient approach, at least in non-rescue cases; see, e.g., *McFarlane* v *EE Caledonian* (above).

Judicial consideration of the nature of the incident has in recent times taken a rather different perspective, the effect of which is to further limit what is regarded as actionable harm. In *Alcock*, Lord Keith refers to shock 'in the sense of a sudden assault upon the senses' [1994] 4 All ER 907 at 915. That would seem to preclude recognisable psychiatric injury brought about over a period of time, albeit a short one. This may be so, even where the harm itself is identical to that which would have been produced by a sudden shock; see the recent decision of the Court of Appeal in *Taylorson* v *Shieldness Produce Ltd* (above).

Similarly in *Taylor* v *Somerset Health Authority* (above), Auld J took the view that any duty of care owed to the wife of a patient did not extend to nervous shock sustained as a result of the patient's sudden death from heart disease which the hospital had negligently failed to detect. This sort of event did not fit within the recognised category of 'some external traumatic event caused by the defendant's breach of duty'.

Finally, it is interesting to reflect upon the decision in *Attia* v *British Gas* [1988] QB 304. The case dealt with the novel point as to whether or not a duty of care might extend to a situation in which a plaintiff suffered nervous shock at the sight of the destruction of her home by fire caused by the defendant's negligence. A similar question was raised (though it did not fall to be decided) in *Owens* v *Liverpool Corporation* [1939] 1 KB 394, when Mackinnon LJ at pp. 399–400 asked:

if real injury has genuinely been caused by shock from apprehension as to something less important than human life (for example, the life of a beloved dog), can the sufferer recover no damages for the injury he, or perhaps oftener she has sustained?

The decision in *Attia* predates *Alcock* and though no adverse comment was made upon it in the House of Lords in that case, its authority may be in question given the much more restrictive approach taken in *Alcock* and subsequent cases.

ILLUSTRATIVE QUESTION

Dan, an airline pilot and employee of C Airlines Ltd, negligently crashes an airliner whilst attempting a landing at Bogpool Airport. All the passengers and crew abroad the aircraft are killed in the horrific explosion and fire which ensue. Consider the possible liability of C Airlines Ltd to the following persons:

(a)   Freda, who is at the airport to meet her cousin who is aboard the aircraft. Freda witnesses the accident from the crowded spectators' balcony. She is admitted to hospital in a state of shock.

(b)   Percy, who is on his way to the airport to collect his wife who is aboard the fateful flight. He hears of the accident on his car radio. On reaching the airport he can see a cloud of smoke rising from out on the runway. He is prevented from going any closer to the scene by security officials. Gradually he realises from conversations around him that all on board may have perished. Two hours later he identifies his wife's badly damaged body in the mortuary. As a result of his experiences he suffers a serious nervous disorder and is now unable to work.

(c)   Jim, an airport worker, rushes to the scene intent on giving assistance but faints at the sight of the badly burnt and dismembered bodies scattered on the runway. Jim now suffers from post traumatic stress disorder (PTSD).

(d)   Albert, an air traffic controller under whose control the aircraft was landing, witnesses the accident from the control tower and suffers a serious nervous disorder as a result. Albert has only recently recovered from a nervous breakdown as a result of overworking.

COMMENTARY

Whilst it is not difficult to structure an answer to this particular question, nevertheless we would suggest that the preparation of a rough plan would be useful from the point of view of identifying the various issues and dealing with them in a sensible order in each of the possible actions against C Airlines Ltd (C) by Freda (F), Percy (P), Jim (J) and Albert (A). In particular, care should be taken to avoid needless repetitive discussion of issues which may arise in more than one of the possible actions against C Ltd.

Before considering these possible actions in any detail there are two preliminary issues which need to be disposed of. First, the question clearly states that Dan, the pilot, is an employee of C. The question of the liability of C for the actions of Dan can be suitably dealt with fairly briefly by stating the normal rule that employers are generally vicariously liable for the torts of their employees which the latter commit within the course of their employment. It would therefore be inappropriate to engage in speculation as to what the legal position of C might be if Dan were an independent contractor. As to the second point, the question states that Dan negligently crashes the aircraft. Negligence in a legal sense presupposes a duty of care. Undoubtedly, C would owe such a duty to the passengers and members of the crew through its employee, Dan. However, the examiner in such a question would not by the use of the word 'negligently', presuppose the existence of a duty of care in law to any of the prospective plaintiffs identified in the question. That is itself the central point the question requires the student to consider. What the examiner is trying to do by using the term 'negligently' in this fashion, is to avoid speculation by the student about unstated facts which may affect the issue of breach of a duty of care, for example, was it an emergency landing? Accordingly, we would advise students to avoid speculation on the issue of breach and to concentrate upon the issue of duty.

Freda (F) v C Airlines Ltd (C)

Consideration of the possible liability of C will inevitably involve the question of any duty of care owed to F. An acceptable way to commence the discussion would be to ask whether or not the harm sustained by F falls within the category of legally recognised harm. Whilst the question states that F is admitted to hospital 'in a state of shock' it stops short of identifying with any precision what harm has actually befallen her. A careful reading of the question shows the position of F is quite different in this respect from that of the other plaintiffs. An explanation of what constitutes actionable harm is called for, and in this context would need to deal with the well established but difficult distinction which is drawn between emotional disturbances such as grief, sorrow and anguish as opposed to recognised psychiatric injury or illness. Great emphasis is placed upon this distinction in all the reported cases. One might cite, for example, Lord Bridge in *McLoughlin* v *O'Brian* [1983] 1 AC 410, at p. 431:

[T]he first hurdle which a plaintiff claiming damages of the kind in question must surmount is to establish that he is suffering, not merely grief, distress or any other normal emotion, but a positive psychiatric illness.

It is no doubt extremely common for people to suffer grief and sorrow and even transient shock as a result of witnessing a serious accident. It seems reasonably clear from the above statement and from dicta in other cases, for example, Lord Denning MR in *Hinz* v *Berry* [1970] 2 QB at p. 42 and Kennedy J in *Dulieu* v *White & Sons* [1901] 2 KB 669 at p. 730, that damages are not generally recoverable for this kind of emotional disturbance. If this is all that F has suffered, then there is no cause of action. A student who was able to explain by reference to the case law that this distinction is perhaps not as clear cut as it may appear to be, would undoubtedly impress the examiner. For example, grief may itself be of such an order that it is recognisable as a psychiatric illness. In the litigation following the disaster involving the *Herald of Free Enterprise*, 'pathological grief' was held to be actionable psychiatric damage (see *Re the Herald of Free Enterprise*, *The Guardian*, 2 May 1991). Other cases which perhaps deserve mention in this context would include *Kralj* v *McGrath* [1986] 1 All ER 54 and *Whitmore* v *Euroways Express Coaches Ltd* (1984) *The Times*, 4 May.

Assuming that F has sustained actionable damage, it should then be pointed out that to cause such injury even by conduct which is negligent will not result in liability unless the defendant (C) owed the plaintiff (F) a duty of care. Even if the injury to F was foreseeable on the facts, it does not necessarily follow that a duty of care in law is owed to her by C.

In dealing with the issue of the duty of care towards the various plaintiffs, we should, following the decision of the House of Lords in *Alcock*, accept that the restrictions identified in the speech of Lord Wilberforce, which we summarised above, are to apply even to the point of excluding recovery for foreseeable harm.

A further word of explanation as to the possible structure of an answer is perhaps appropriate here. It would be perfectly possible to approach the question by considering how each of the restrictions applies to the various plaintiffs. Using this approach one would consider, e.g., the requirement of the relationship between the victim and the plaintiff. In this commentary we have structured our consideration of the question around the individual claims of the plaintiffs. We would advise that students adopt this approach in answering this kind of question. By so doing we place greater emphasis upon the combination of the restrictions applicable to the individual plaintiff. This is, in our view, the real key to the existence in law of a duty of care.

The facts of the question show that F has witnessed the accident itself with her own unaided senses but from a position some distance from the accident. The fact that a plaintiff sees the accident or the aftermath through his or her own unaided senses may not of itself be sufficient to render foreseeable, injury to him or her by shock, see *Hay (or Bourhill)* v *Young* (above). This decision is unlikely to be applied on this point where there is a close family relationship between plaintiff and victim. Support for this view is to be found in *King* v *Phillips* [1953] 1 QB 429. In that case Denning LJ expressed the view that the distance between the plaintiff mother and her child whom she thought had been injured, was immaterial. Thus, despite her position in the spectator's balcony, which may be some distance away, F would almost certainly be regarded as being sufficiently proximate to the event in terms of time and place. Furthermore, as the question indicates, the event is one of an horrific nature quite beyond the normal experience. A good answer should explain that the nature of the event is a relevant consideration, see, e.g., our earlier quotation from the judgment of Lord Porter in *Hay (or Bourhill)* v *Young*.

The real point of uncertainty affecting the question as to whether or not C owed F any duty of care in law, concerns the relationship between F and the victim, her cousin. The discussion of this issue should emphasise that the dicta of Lord Wilberforce in *McLoughlin* did not preclude the possibility of relationships other than parents/spouses being sufficient in this respect. His Lordship suggested that:

> other cases involving less close relationships must be very carefully scrutinised. . . . The claim, in any case, has to be judged in the light of the other factors, such as proximity to the scene in time and place, and the nature of the accident. ([1983] 1 AC 410 at p. 422.)

As we indicated above, the consideration of these 'other factors' seems favourable to F's claim. Following the decision in *Alcock* it is now clear that a duty of care may extend to wider familial relationships provided they are relationships with close ties of love and affection.

Whilst a student can only speculate as to the quality of the relationship between F and her cousin, there are two points upon which an examiner may legitimately expect some observation. First, are there any indications in the judgments as to how close these ties of love and affection need to be? Does the relationship have to be as close in this sense as that which might exist between spouses in a happy and successful marriage? There is some suggestion of this in the judgment of Lord Ackner in *Alcock* [1991] 4 All ER 907 at p. 919 which might be invoked by a court bent upon a restrictive interpretation of *Alcock* which seems the present trend.

Secondly, it would appear from *Alcock* that the burden of persuasion in such a case would lie with F, as the rebuttable presumption in favour of the existence of such ties appears to be confined to parents, spouses and (per Lord Keith, [1994] 4 All ER 907 at p. 914) fiancés.

Percy (P) v C Airlines Ltd (C)

The facts of the problem raise a number of issues which need to be dealt with, but not all require the same depth of discussion. For example, in the light of the earlier consideration of this matter, it would be sufficient to indicate that close ties of love and affection as between P and his wife would be presumed.

It should be pointed out that for the purposes of further argument it is assumed that there is no evidence to the contrary to rebut that presumption.

Similarly, the facts make it fairly clear that P has suffered what is likely to be regarded as actionable psychiatric injury and reference to the earlier discussion on this issue in the context of F's claim would be sufficient and a sensible strategy.

The most troublesome questions in any claim by P are likely to be:

(a) What constitutes the aftermath?
(b) Was P sufficiently proximate to the aftermath in time and space?

Before considering these matters it is appropriate to remind students that it may be impossible to reach any firm conclusions on such issues simply because of uncertainty in the law. Examiners do not expect students to resolve such uncertainty but to demonstrate an understanding of the state of the law.

What constitutes the aftermath?
We can see from the facts that P satisfies the 'own unaided senses rule' in that he saw something of the events and was not merely reliant on information received via the radio or the conversations amongst third parties at the airport. It should be pointed out that no duty would be owed if those communications were the sole link with the events and supportive reference should be made to *Alcock, Ravenscroft* v *Rederiaktiebolaget Translantic* and *Hevican* v *Ruane* (above). P did not see the accident itself however and would therefore have to argue that what he did see constituted the immediate aftermath, sufficient to bring him within a duty of care owed to him by C.

The analysis of P's claim should recognise that his argument might be based either upon the scenes at the airport itself, on the identification of the body at the mortuary or on a combination of both.

In dealing with these two possibilities it might be useful to begin by quoting Lord Wilberforce in *McLoughlin*, that a duty may be owed to 'one who from close proximity comes immediately upon the aftermath'.

With regard to the scene at the airport, this is clearly the immediate aftermath and P arrives on the scene very shortly after the accident. But what did P actually see? We are told that he saw the smoke rising from a distance. We would hope that students would recognise this as one of the weaker points of P's claim by comparison with *McLoughlin*. In that case much emphasis was placed upon the presence of the victims before the plaintiff in circumstances in which their injuries and distress were clearly visible. Additional reference should be made to *Alcock* and the importance which was attached to this particular feature of *McLoughlin* by the House of Lords in that case. An observation that the decision in *McLoughlin* might be distinguishable, and therefore of no assistance to P, would certainly be in order.

The identification of the body at the mortuary must be considered as an alternative. The facts of the question indicate that P's claim is somewhat stronger in the sense of what he actually saw (the badly burnt body of his wife). The main point of difficulty here is whether, and if so, in what circumstances, the identification of bodies can be a part of the immediate aftermath so as to bring claimants such as P within a duty of care.

We indicated earlier in this chapter that the reasoning of the House of Lords in *Alcock* on this matter was somewhat diverse. A good answer should demonstrate an awareness of that and the possible implications. The various reasons given for the failure of the claims included lack of sufficient relationship (per Lord Keith), distinguishable here, and lack of sufficient proximity in terms of time and distance (per Lord Ackner). The decision in *McLoughlin* was distinguished by Lord Jauncey on the additional grounds that the victims in *McLoughlin* were in the same state as they would have been at the scene of the accident itself and suggests that the purpose of a visit to a victim must be to rescue or to offer comfort.

This latter point is taken by Auld J to exclude the plaintiff from any duty of care in *Taylor* v *Somerset Health Authority* (above). In his view the purpose of the plaintiff's visit to the mortuary was to settle her disbelief as to his reported death and was not capable of being part of any possible immediate aftermath. If this view is correct than we should recognise that it may exclude the possibility of claims based upon the identification of bodies as in P's case.

The final argument P might raise is that a whole series of events both at the airport and at the mortuary constituted the immediate aftermath and his injury is the direct and foreseeable result of those events. Whilst at first sight this argument may have some appeal, it may well fail because of the view that the injury must be caused by a traumatic event which creates 'a sudden assault upon the senses'. This will exclude from any duty of care those who are injured through a gradual process even though this may be entirely foreseeable.

The Court of Appeal in *Taylorson* v *Shieldness Produce Ltd* (above) adopted this line of reasoning. In so doing the court was not persuaded to follow the Australian common law decision in *Jaensch* v *Coffey* (1984) 54 ALR 417 to the contrary.

Jim (J) v *C Airlines Ltd (C)*

The discussion of J's claim should deal first, and rather briefly, with the kind of psychological harm which J has sustained. This may be achieved partly by reference to the discussion of this issue in F's claim (above).

The main point requiring discussion is whether or not J may be treated as a rescuer. In dealing with this reference should be made to the cases in which a duty of care has been established with regard to rescuers, e.g., *Chadwick* v

British Railways Board [1967] 1 WLR 912. In that case the plaintiff became psycho-neurotic as a result of his voluntary involvement following the Lewisham train disaster, a particularly horrific rail accident with many dead and injured. But the circumstances in which a rescuer may be owed a duty are not confined to events on this scale (see *Galt* v *British Railways Board* (1983) 133 NLJ 870).

These and other cases demonstrate a willingness to recognise a duty of care towards rescuers. Their presence is readily foreseeable and the fact that that in itself is sufficient is an indication of the influence of policy considerations.

These cases have been confirmed as good law by the House of Lords in *McLoughlin* and more recently in *Alcock*. In those cases the active involvement of the plaintiff in giving aid and comfort is obvious. Lord Oliver in *Alcock* recognised these as a category of cases separate from others in which the plaintiff is the mere passive and unwilling witness of injury caused to others in which there needs to be a close relationship of love and affection between plaintiff and the person injured or in peril.

The illustrative question is deliberately worded to raise the possibility that J fainted before he was able to attempt to offer assistance. This should serve as another reminder of the need to read questions carefully.

Assume for argument sake that J does faint before he can render assistance, students have to be prepared to argue points of this kind. So rather than simply saying 'J may or may not be treated as a rescuer', argue the point. Examiners look for, and reward, what is after all one of the basic lawyering skills.

To that end it should be pointed out that whether or not a person is to be treated as a rescuer falling within a duty of care is essentially a question of fact. This will be determined by the extent of their involvement and consequent risk of injury through shock. In *McFarlane* v *EE Caledonian* (above) the Court of Appeal rejected the plaintiff's claim as a rescuer on the grounds that his involvement in the rescue of workers escaping from the fire on Piper Alpha was minimal, and exposed him to little if any risk of psychiatric injury.

The decision in *McFarlane* can be distinguished on the facts. J has clearly exposed himself to the risk of psychiatric injury by going right to the horrendous scene. The difficulty is that he was not able to be actively involved in offering aid or comfort as were the plaintiffs in the other rescue cases. It could however be argued in J's favour that his noble intentions separate him from nosey spectators to whom no duty would be owed.

Should this argument fail and were J to be regarded merely as a passive spectator, students should be prepared to put forward an alternative argument. J may still be owed a duty of care despite the absence of any relationship between himself and any of the victims. In *Alcock* the possible existence of a duty towards a 'stranger' was recognised by Lords Keith, Ackner and Oliver (see [1994] 4 All ER 907 at pp. 914, 919 and 930, respectively). Their Lordships contemplated that this duty might exist where a spectator witnesses a particularly horrendous scene, e.g., a petrol tanker careering out of control into a school in session and bursting into flames.

The decision in *McFarlane* is of considerable interest not simply because it considered and rejected this argument on the facts. In so doing Stuart-Smith LJ, who gave the sole judgment in the Court of Appeal, clearly rejects in principle that a duty of care could be owed to a stranger (see [1994] 2 All ER 1 at 14).

Albert (A) v C Airlines Ltd (C)

Any claim by A to be owed a duty of care by C appears weak in two respects. These should be the central concern of the discussion. Situated in the control tower A has a good view of the horrendous event, though there might be some argument as to whether or not he was sufficiently proximate in physical terms. The major doubts as to the likelihood of the success of his claim arise from the assumed absence of any relationship between himself and anyone involved in the accident. His previous medical history suggests that he may be especially vulnerable to injury through shock and thus an unforeseeable victim to whom no duty would be owed.

The analysis of A's claim should emphasise that the absence of any relationship between A and the victims of the accident may not be fatal to his claim. He may be able to bring himself within the first category of cases identified by Lord Oliver in *Alcock* (see [1992] 4 All ER 907 at 923) which covers shock to those who are actively involved in the events themselves. As we indicated above, this category includes rescuers, but it may also include others as illustrated by the decision in *Dooley* v *Cammell Laird & Co. Ltd* [1951] 1 Lloyd's Rep 271. This decision was approved by the Court of Appeal in *Jones* v *Wright* [1991] 3 All ER 88, though the basis of the approval was not entirely clear. Was the existence of the duty based on the fact that the plaintiff was an employee of one of the defendants or did the duty arise on the different ground that the plaintiff was actually involved in the accident which caused his shock?

In *Alcock*, the decision in *Dooley* was regarded as good law by Lord Oliver alongside the rescue cases on the basis of the plaintiff's active involvement in the events (see [1992] 4 All ER 907 at p. 923). The importance of this should be emphasised since it is most unlikely that A is an employee of C Airlines Ltd. The second major issue arises from the fact that A has previously suffered a nervous breakdown and may, therefore, have a predisposition towards injury through shock. The question which arises is, assuming he is more susceptible than the normal person, would a duty of care be owed to him in the light of the fact that such susceptibility was not foreseeable? The cases are riddled with statements to the effect that the duty of care is only owed to a person of 'customary phlegm' (the origin of this rather unpleasant term appears to be the judgment of Lord Porter in *Bourhill* v *Young* [1943] AC 92 at p. 117). However, if in the circumstances of a case a person of normal disposition would have sustained harm through shock by reason of the defendant's negligence, then it matters not that the plaintiff was especially susceptible to this type of harm. This appears to be a well-established principle and can be detected in cases in other areas, see, for example, *Robinson* v *Kilvert* (1889) 41 ChD 88 (damage to property by alleged nuisance). See also the decision of the High Court on nervous shock, *Brice* v *Brown* [1984] 1 All ER 997, which reinforces the point.

If, however, a court concludes on the facts that a person of normal disposition would not have sustained harm through the shock, then no duty of care would be owed to the especially sensitive plaintiff as in the recent decision of the Court of Appeal in *McFarlane* v *EE Caledonian* (above). There seems here to be a conflict with the rule that a tortfeasor must take his victim as he finds him ('eggshell skull' rule). This is a difficult relationship to resolve, but perhaps best explained by recognising that the 'eggshell skull' rule is essentially concerned with the issue of remoteness of damage and the extent of harm suffered by a plaintiff to whom it has been established that a duty of care is owed (see *Smith* v *Leech Brain & Co. Ltd* [1962] 2 QB 405).

CONCLUSION

Apart from summarising briefly the prospects of success of the various plaintiffs, a student could beneficially make some concluding observations upon the present state of the law and the desirability of legislative intervention. In both *McLoughlin* and *Alcock* the House of Lords has made reference to the existence of the Australian legislation and there are some clear expressions of dissatisfaction with the law as it stands. The inclusion of brief observations as to how the plaintiffs in our illustrative question might fare under that legislation would undoubtedly gain credit with the examiner.

ILLUSTRATIVE QUESTION

Try this one yourself!

Consider whether B Bus Company owes a duty of care to any of the persons injured in the circumstances outlined below.

A serious accident occurred when a double decker bus carrying school children collided with a low bridge, killing or injuring several children. The bus was owned and operated by B Bus Company. Fred, the driver, who was new to the area, had been ordered to use that particular route due to the closure of the normal route for road repairs.

(a)   Fred, the driver, who, though not physically injured, sat dazed at the wheel of the bus until taken away in an ambulance. He now suffers from vivid recurring nightmares and has been unable to work since the accident.

(b)   Violet, the wife of Fred, has a previous history of nervous disorder. She suffered shock when told of the accident by a policeman who called at her home 30 minutes after the accident.

(c)   Mr Thrashem, the headmaster of the school from which the children had been collected, learned of the accident almost immediately by telephone. He straight away drove to the scene and comforted some of the injured children in an ambulance on the journey to the local hospital. He now suffers from post traumatic stress disorder.

(d)   Samantha, who was being driven home in her mum's car which was immediately behind the bus when the accident happened. She feared for the safety of her lifelong friend Kirsty who invariably sat on the front seat on the upper deck of the bus. Her mother drove her away from the scene in an hysterical state. She too now suffers from post traumatic stress disorder.

SELECTED READING

Teff, 'Liability for Negligently Inflicted Nervous Shock' (1983) 99 LQR 100.
Trindade, 'The Principles Governing the Recovery of Damages for Negligently Caused Nervous Shock' [1986] CLJ 476.

9 NEGLIGENCE 6: ECONOMIC LOSS

INTRODUCTION

The student would perhaps find it useful if we began this chapter by defining what is meant by the lawyer's term 'economic loss', because most losses are in a sense 'economic' in that the reparation most frequently available under the law is pecuniary or financial in its nature, namely damages. The term 'economic loss' as used in the narrower sense, is loss which is not consequent upon any injury to the plaintiff or any damage to property in which he has a sufficient possessory or proprietary interest. Perhaps two illustrations will serve to show what is meant by what is commonly called 'pure' economic loss and the potential scale on which such losses may result from one single inadvertent act, given the complex interrelationship of financial interests in a modern industrial and commercial society.

Illustration 1

Suppose a virus escapes from some research institute which infects cattle in the immediate locality. The cattle have to be destroyed and all movement of cattle is restricted for six months until the virus is eliminated. Assuming negligence on the part of the institute, is it to be held liable not merely for the foreseeable damage to property, namely the cattle, but also for the foreseeable damage to financial interests which follow from the ban? The local cattle auctioneer will no doubt be deprived, albeit temporarily, of his livelihood. Haulage firms specialising in the movement of cattle, garages where the drivers would have bought their diesel and even the cafe where the drivers would have bought their bacon sandwiches are but a few of the businesses which would, in some measure, sustain financial losses in the obvious knock-on effect. These financial losses are not consequential upon any injury to their persons or damage to their property, but yet are clearly foreseeable. The facts in our hypothetical situation are essentially those in *Weller & Co.* v *Foot & Mouth Disease Research Institute* [1966] 1 QB 569, with some embellishment, in which the action by an auctioneer for loss of business was unsuccessful.

Illustration 2

Our second illustration is somewhat anecdotal, but we believe should bring home to the student with considerable force just how vast is the scope for potential claims if the foreseeability principle under *Donoghue* v *Stevenson* [1932] AC 562 is applied without restriction to allow the recovery of 'pure' economic loss.

In 1977 as a result of negligence the whole of New York City and its surrounding areas were deprived of electricity. Ten million residents were without power for 25 hours. Apparently, more than 180 law suits were filed against the persons responsible. The loss to business was incalculable even if one only takes account of the loss of production and profits thereon, to those firms which sustained no damage to their property whatsoever.

The recovery of economic loss is well established in English law, particularly where such loss is inflicted *intentionally*. Examples of this would include the torts of deceit, conspiracy, procuring/inducing breach of contract and passing off. The question with which this chapter is concerned is the extent to which *unintentionally* inflicted economic loss is recoverable in the tort of negligence, a tort which is of much wider application than those mentioned above.

Whilst the decision in *Hedley Byrne & Co. Ltd* v *Heller & Partners Ltd* [1964] AC 465 recognised a much wider duty of care than had previously existed with regard to economic loss resulting from negligent words, that development was not embraced by the Misrepresentation Act 1967. Liability for negligent words may therefore arise under either (or both) the common law and the statutory provisions. There are a number of significant differences between these two heads of liability. Most notable perhaps is that liability under the 1967 Act is confined within a 'privity of contract' rule embodied in s. 2(1), a restriction which was expressly rejected in the common law in *Hedley Byrne*. The study of law as an academic discipline has led to a good deal of artificial classification and, notwithstanding the continuing erosion of the doctrine of privity of contract, the law of torts and the law of contract continue to be taught and examined with separate syllabuses in many institutions. Liability under the Misrepresentation Act 1967 is conventionally taught within the law of contract syllabus whilst the common law liability remains firmly within the province of torts. We have in this chapter essentially confined ourselves to a discussion of the common law liability with only brief comments as to the liability which may arise under the 1967 Act.

The considerable development in the common law following the decision in *Hedley Byrne* is such that it is most unlikely to be ignored in any torts syllabus or indeed in any examination paper. There is little doubt that close study of this area will pay dividends at examination time.

SUBSTANTIVE DIFFICULTIES

Students will be aware that there has been, in recent times a substantial amount of case law on this subject, in which the tide of recovery has ebbed and flowed. A number of those cases were included in our discussion of the notional duty of care in chapter 4. Before considering the circumstances in which economic loss is recoverable we must first attempt to distil from the cases a more precise definition of what constitutes economic loss as opposed to, e.g., property damage.

The so-called 'general' rule which restricts the recovery of economic loss in negligence was postulated by Lord Penzance in *Simpson & Co.* v *Thomson* (1887) 3 App Cas 279 at 289. Though the sweeping authority of that obiter dicta was not accepted by the House of Lords in *Hedley Byrne* v *Heller and Partners* [1964] AC 465, it has been accepted as being a rule of general, though not universal, application in a number of recent cases. As we indicated earlier, the essence of the rule is that economic loss which is not consequent upon personal injury or damage to property in which the plaintiff has a sufficient possessory or proprietary interest, is not recoverable under the broad principle of *Donoghue* v *Stevenson* [1932] AC 562. Students must not assume that this means that such loss is therefore not recoverable at all, for it may be recovered in certain exceptional situations where there exists between the parties an especially close proximate relationship, as in *Hedley Byrne* (above).

In order to try to make some sense of the complex state of the present law we need to recognise that there are, broadly, three types of case which cause difficulties. In these cases the courts may be reluctant to allow the claim either out of their concern to avoid imposing indeterminate liability on the defendant, or because of the effect which such claims might have upon the established rules of the law of contract if they were to be allowed. In the first two categories of cases examined the arguments concern whether the damage is to be regarded as property damage (and recoverable under *Donogbue* v *Stevenson*) or economic loss, in which case the loss is only recoverable in exceptional circumstances. In the third type of case there is no doubt as to the nature of the loss sustained, and the argument centres upon the question of whether or not there existed a special close proximate relationship between the plaintiff and the defendant sufficient to permit recovery.

The first category includes those cases in which the plaintiff's loss is quite clearly consequential upon damage to property, but where the plaintiff may not have a sufficient interest in the property damaged so as to recover successfully under the broad foresight principle. Perhaps the most obvious example of such a claim failing is that of the plaintiff auctioneers in *Weller* v *Foot & Mouth Disease Research Institute*, to which we referred in our earlier illustration. Other cases would include those in which lost profits are claimed by businesses due solely to the delay in the restoration of utility services which have been negligently disrupted; see *Spartan Steel & Alloys Ltd* v *Martin & Co. (Contractors) Ltd* [1972] 3 WLR 502 CA, *SCM (UK) Ltd* v *W. J. Whittall & Son Ltd* [1970] 3 WLR 694. Students should not be shy of reading some of the older cases such as *Cattle* v *Stockton Waterworks* (1875) LR 10 QB 453 or *Anglo-Algerian Steamship Co. Ltd* v *The Houlder Line Ltd* [1908] 1 KB 659, for they provide excellent illustrations of the variety of situations in which such losses may arise.

The really difficult cases are those in which the plaintiff has some kind of interest in the damaged property and the point in question is whether that interest is sufficient to enable him to claim successfully the losses consequential thereon, under *Donoghue* v *Stevenson*. Students need, therefore, to address the question as to what kind of interest will suffice in this respect. Whilst the starting point of the investigation of this issue may be the dictum of Lord Penzance in *Simpson* v *Thomson* (above), there has been a good number of subsequent cases which tell us a great deal more. Quite a number of these cases have been concerned with the different forms of ship charter. We recognise that students with no knowledge of shipping law will experience some difficulty in reading these cases in view of the unfamiliar concepts and terminology employed therein. We would suggest that a sufficient general understanding of the issue in this context may be derived from the careful reading of two cases — *Konstantinidis* v *World Tankers Corp. (The World Harmony)* [1965] 2 WLR 1275 and *Candlewood Navigation Corporation Ltd* v *Mitsui OSK Lines Ltd* [1985] 3 WLR 381 PC. The latter case concerns a curious arrangement under which the owner let the boat to another party under a time charter. The boat was then let back to the owner under what was termed a 'bare boat' charter. The action was brought by the owner in his capacity as bare boat charterer, which interest was insufficient to support the action for financial losses incurred as a result of damage to the ship.

Several other cases in which this issue has been raised involve the esoteric niceties of C.I.F. and other special forms of export sale contracts. Unless students are more specifically directed, we would again suggest that it is not necessary to wade through the substantial body of existing case law. A general appreciation of the application of Lord Penzance's rule in these types of case may be gleaned from studying the decision in *Leigh and Sillavan Ltd* v *Aliakmon Shipping Co. Ltd (The Aliakmon)* [1985] 2 All ER 44 CA, [1986] 2 All

ER 145 HL; see also *Transcontainer Express Ltd* v *Custodian Security Ltd* [1988] 1 Lloyd's Rep 128.

Two other recent decisions are useful in the sense that they help throw some light on the kind of possessory interest in the damaged property which might suffice in other areas, see *Nacap Ltd* v *Moffat Plant Ltd* [1987] SLT 221, *North Scottish Helicopters* v *United Technologies Corp.* [1988] SLT 77.

In our second category are those cases in which the plaintiff clearly has a sufficient interest in the property in question, the value of which is diminished as a result of the defendant's breach. This diminution may be regarded as economic loss rather than damage to property as such. This distinction has been drawn in cases concerning both real and personal property. The underlying rationale seems to be essentially concerned with preventing the established rules of contract law being undermined by developments in the tort of negligence.

An action in tort by a consumer against a manufacturer for the diminution in value of safe but shoddy goods is regarded as an action for economic loss rather than property damage. Similarly under the most recent decision of the House of Lords in *D & F Estates Ltd* v *Church Commissioners (and others)* [1988] 3 WLR 368, the cost of repairing the goods is to be so regarded, even where that expense is incurred in obviating discovered defects which render the goods dangerous. This decision, together with those in *Muirhead* v *Industrial Tank Specialities* [1986] QB 507 and *MIS Aswan Engineering Ltd* v *Lupdine Ltd* [1987] 1 WLR 1, illustrate how fine the dividing line between the two categories of loss may be. The distinction may be equally difficult to draw in other areas. In the previous editions we posed the question as to the nature of the loss sustained in the local authority cases such as *Anns* v *Merton* (above). Was it physical damage to P's property, or 'physical' in a different sense, namely, the damage represented a threat to health and safety? On the other hand it could be argued that the remedial costs and the diminution in value of the property were merely economic loss and recoverable only in 'exceptional' cases. In *Murphy* (above) the issue was conclusively settled that the loss was pure economic loss.

Some of the losses caused to the owners and occupiers of premises by the negligent exercise of power conferred by a statute, the object of which is public safety, had hitherto been regarded as damage to property. This was so provided the state of the premises posed a threat to safety. In the absence of any threat to safety, the loss was regarded as economic and its prevention was not within the duty of care associated with the exercise of such statutory powers; see *Governors of the Peabody Donation Fund* v *Sir Lindsay Parkinson & Co. Ltd* [1985] AC 210; *Investors in Industry* v *South Bedfordshire District Council* [1986] QB 1034. *Murphy* departed from the decision in *Anns* and overruled the Court of Appeal in *Dutton* v *Bognor Regis UDC* [1972] 1 QB 373, and all cases subsequent to and based on the *Anns'* decision.

Where, on the other hand, such damage is caused by the negligence of others involved in the construction of buildings, e.g., builders, architects, etc., the costs of repair are regarded as mere economic loss and irrecoverable except possibly where some special close relationship exists between the parties, even though the expenditure which is incurred is necessary to render the premises safe; see *D & F Estates* v *Church Commissioners* (above). The line taken by the House of Lords in this case, that once a defect is discovered it is no longer a source of danger, looks like an exercise in semantics. The underlying rationale seems quite clearly to be that of protecting the established rules of the law of contract.

In our third category, as we shall see, the cases do recognise that some forms of economic loss are recoverable within very narrow limits, but it should not be thought that all forms of economic loss are recoverable even within these narrow limits. In the cases so far decided recovery has been allowed, for example, of the loss of expectation by a beneficiary under a will (see *Ross* v *Caunters* [1980] Ch 297, approved by the Court of Appeal in *White* v *Jones* [1993] 3 All ER 481 and the House of Lords (3–2 majority only) (1995) *The Times*, 17 February) and of remedial expenditure incurred in connection with defective property where there was no attendant risk to health or safety (see *Junior Books Ltd* v *Veitchi Co. Ltd* [1983] 1 AC 520). Whether loss of profits *simpliciter* is recoverable remains open to considerable doubt. Furthermore, as we saw in chapter 4, considerations of policy adverse to the plaintiff's case may be such that the courts are unwilling to impose liability despite the existence of a special relationship between the parties.

One difficulty in this area is that there appear to be two distinct lines of authority under which economic loss may be recovered. The first of these is the principle of detrimental reliance established in *Hedley Byrne* (above) and developed in numerous subsequent cases. The principle was formulated essentially to deal with liability for negligent statements though it may extend to other forms of negligent conduct provided the central element of reasonable reliance as between plaintiff and defendant is present. It is this requirement of detrimental reliance which renders the principle inappropriate in cases such as *Ross* v *Caunters* (above) and a wide variety of other cases in which the defendant's negligence is the clear cause of the plaintiff's financial loss even in the absence of reliance. Recovery of economic loss in these other types of case was, however recognised to some extent through the application of the by-now-familiar but discredited two-stage approach of Lord Wilberforce in *Anns* v *Merton London Borough Council* [1978] AC 728. This approach was employed not only in those situations where the *Hedley Byrne* principle was inappropriate but it was adopted as an alternative in certain cases which arguably fell within that principle, such as *JEB Fasteners Ltd* v *Marks, Bloom & Co.* [1981] 3 All ER 289. So willing were the lower courts to resort to and apply the 'Wilberforce approach', that we were tempted in the first edition to ask whether the *Hedley Byrne* principle has become subsumed within that approach. As we pointed out in chapter 4, there can be little doubt that the appellate courts have now firmly applied the brake to this expansionist trend, with the result that the extent to which economic loss is recoverable outside the *Hedley Byrne* principle is in a state of considerable uncertainty. In the previous edition we were of the view that the decision in *Ross* v *Caunters* (above) was in some doubt. However, as mentioned earlier, the Court of Appeal and the House of Lords in *White* v *Jones* have approved of the principle in the case on the basis that awarding the beneficiary the amount of his or her legacy merely amounts to carrying out the testator's instructions and nothing more. *Junior Books* v *Veitchi* (above) has, in a sense, been brought back into the fold, as it has recently been described as a 'reliance' case (per Lord Keith in *Murphy* v *Brentwood DC* [1990] 3 WLR 414 at p. 427).

In chapter 4 we recognised that the 'Wilberforce approach' appeared to introduce a prima facie duty of care based solely on the foreseeability of damage as between plaintiff and defendant. This seemed to disregard well-established limits, such as the need to establish the existence of an especially close relationship between the parties where economic loss was claimed. The approach also appeared to relegate the influence of precedent, a development which has now been disapproved of and a number of decisions of the lower courts have been reversed in the appellate courts; see *Candlewood* (above), *The Aliakmon* (above) wherein the House of Lords expressly overruled the decision in *Schiffahrt & Kohlen GmbH* v *Chelsea Maritime Ltd (The Irene's Success)* [1982] 1 All ER 218, *Curran* v *Northern Ireland Co-ownership Housing Association Ltd* [1987] 2 All ER 13, HL and finally in *Caparo* v *Dickman* [1990] 2 WLR 358.

In so doing the courts have not confined themselves to the facts of the cases before them, but have expressed strong views as to the recovery of economic loss in general. Lord Brandon suggested that the 'Wilberforce approach' should be used only in 'novel' cases; see *The Aliakmon* [1986] 2 WLR 902 at p. 913. The first stage of the two-stage approach itself was the subject of a substantial and restrictive reinterpretation by the Privy Council in *Yuen Kun-yeu* v *Attorney General of Hong Kong* [1987] 2 All ER 705. In that case the view was taken that Lord Wilberforce had not meant to suggest that foreseeability of the damage alone was sufficient to establish a duty of care in all cases. Rather the notion of sufficient proximity was 'a composite one importing the whole concept of necessary relationship between plaintiff and defendant', per Lord Keith at p. 710. In other cases the courts have held that a duty of care should only be imposed where it is just and reasonable to do so; see *Peabody* (above), *Business Computers International Ltd* v *Registrar of Companies* [1987] 3 All ER 465. In what circumstances is economic loss now recoverable? We attempt to address this issue in the commentary on the illustrative question below.

It would perhaps be helpful at this stage if we pointed to some of the various aspects of the law which apparently cause difficulty under the *Hedley Byrne* principle. One question which is almost always raised in an examination context is by whom is the duty of care owed? Whilst the minority opinion in *Mutual Life & Citizens' Assurance Co. Ltd* v *Evatt* [1971] AC 793 is a refinement of the 'special relationship' adverted to in *Hedley Byrne* itself, nevertheless some degree of uncertainty still remains on this issue. Any statement made on a social occasion would not give rise to a duty of care, nor generally would statements made by private individuals. However, let us consider the position of a private individual selling a second-hand car. Would any statement made by him about the vehicle be regarded as being made 'in a business context' as envisaged by the minority in Evatt's case?

An interesting case is *Chaudry* v *Prahhakar* [1988] 3 All ER 718 as to how far the *Hedley Byrne* principle might reach.

The existence of the duty of care under *Hedley Byrne*, notwithstanding the close proximate relationship between plaintiff and defendant, is subject to policy considerations. The importance of these matters can be seen in chapter 4 in connection with the decisions in *Rondel* v *Worsley* [1969] 1 AC 191 and *Saif Ali* v *Sydney Mitchell & Co.* [1980] AC 198. Whether a duty of care would be held to exist under *Hedley Byrne*, where to do so might subvert the established rules of contract may be open to doubt (cf. discussion later on *Junior Books Ltd* v *Veitchi Co. Ltd* [1983] 1 AC 520).

Reliance is to the *Hedley Byrne* principle what reasonable foresight is to the *Donoghue* v *Stevenson* principle. As we have seen in chapters 4, 5 and 6, there is a good deal of confusion because of the relevance of foresight to issues of duty, breach, causation and remoteness. Similar confusion is to be found in the cases on *Hedley Byrne* on the issue of reliance. The decision in *JEB Fasteners Ltd* v *Marks, Bloom & Co.* [1980] 3 All ER 289 is a good illustration of reliance being examined in terms of causation as well as in terms of duty.

The final issue to be considered under *Hedley Byrne* is to whom is the duty owed? It would appear from the decided cases that the duty is owed to a person or persons whose identity need not necessarily be known to the defendant, but who nevertheless belong to a class of readily *identifiable* persons whose reliance is *foreseen* as opposed to being merely foreseeable. One difficulty that arises, given the ever-present fear of indeterminate liability, is how wide a class of persons is acceptable? The recent *Caparo* case would seem to have adopted a more restrictive approach. The House of Lords took the view that liability was restricted to those situations where *the statement or advice had been given to a known recipient for a specific purpose of which the maker was aware and upon which the recipient had relied to his detriment.* It might be useful to point out that the case was concerned with a proposed takeover of a company based on audited accounts which were alleged to be to some extent incorrect. Whether the principle, bearing in mind the circumstance, is quite as narrow as it might appear from the headnote and judgments is not at all clear.

Our final comment in this section concerns the different types of question through which a student's knowledge and understanding of the issue may be tested. We have chosen an essay-type question in order to convey a broad view of the circumstances in which economic loss is recoverable. The topic might equally be examined by means of a problem-type question. Where this is so, students must ensure that they address the specific points raised therein and suitably confine their wider observations.

ILLUSTRATIVE QUESTION

'In the light of recent cases, discuss the extent to which economic loss is recoverable in the tort of negligence.'

COMMENTARY

The first problem which a student will almost invariably encounter in answering a question of this kind is the sheer volume of cases which may need to be discussed. A careful reading of the question set out above should reveal that we have lightened that particular burden by requiring that the discussion be oriented towards the effects of recent decisions. This style of question is probably quite common given the dynamic nature of law and is certainly appropriate at the present time, given the recent history in this area. We have, however, also chosen this style of question in order to make some fundamental points about examination technique. Any answer to such a question must avoid a lengthy historical analysis, which may have been adopted in lectures and which is often to be found in the learned articles in the legal journals to which students are referred. This should not be taken as an indication that it would be inappropriate to reflect briefly upon the status of some of the older authorities. The main thrust of the answer must, however, be clearly directed to explaining what the law was immediately prior to the recent cases (rather than how it came to be) and their effect thereon.

A second and equally important point needs to be made here. Earlier in the chapter we recognised that there were two distinct lines of authority under which economic loss may be recovered, i.e., under *Hedley Byrne* or the now discredited 'Wilberforce approach'. A rough plan of an answer, including the recent cases listed under these heads, would immediately reveal that the majority have been concerned with the scope of the 'Wilberforce approach'. However, there have been several recent cases on the scope of *Hedley Byrne*, not least *Caparo*, but also the decision of the House of Lords in *Harris* v *Wyre District Council* [1989] 2 All ER 514.

Regurgitating the details of the recent cases in some haphazard fashion is unlikely to impress your examiner. The structure of an answer to this type of question is extremely important. The structure itself demonstrates a certain level of understanding of the case law. This may require order to be produced out of chaos. Your efforts to that end will certainly not be lost on the examiner.

Common sense would suggest that a student should begin by demonstrating a clear understanding of what is regarded as economic loss as distinct from property damage. The basic definition, i.e., that it is financial loss which is not a consequence of injury to the plaintiff or damage to his property, would need to be expanded upon by way of an explanation of the cases to which we referred earlier in this chapter.

The first type of case which needs to be dealt with is that in which the plaintiff's loss is consequential upon damage to property, but his interest in that property is called into question. Students will appreciate that there are several recent cases which touch upon this issue and it would be necessary, under examination conditions, to summarise the upshot of these cases in a fairly brief fashion along the following lines.

Where the plaintiff's loss is consequent upon damage to property in which the plaintiff has no proprietary (or insufficient possessory) interest, his loss is categorised as 'economic'. Such loss is not recoverable simply because it is both foreseeable and direct. The principles enunciated in *Donoghue* v *Stevenson* (above) are not applicable to such cases. This remains true even though the plaintiff is the *intended owner* at the time the property is damaged; see, for example, *The Aliakmon* (1986). Numerous other cases illustrate the application of this principle in a wide variety of situations, including what might be termed the 'shipping cases' such as *Candlewood* and the 'utilities' cases such as *Spartan Steel* v *Martin*.

Mere physical possession by the plaintiff of the damaged goods, e.g., by virtue of contract, may not of itself suffice to enable the plaintiff to claim for his consequential losses under *Donoghue* v *Stevenson*. In the light of the recent decisions in *Nacap* v *Moffatt* and the *North Scottish Helicopters* case, it would appear that physical possession under the terms of a contract for very limited purposes, e.g., installing goods, as in *Nacap*, is not sufficient. On the other hand, a person in possession under a lease or even a bailment at will, which confers a substantial degree of freedom of use of the property which is damaged, will suffice, as was the position in the *North Scottish Helicopters* case.

Students will observe that the style we have adopted here serves to present an 'overview' of the case law. But note also how we were a little more specific in respect of the two last mentioned and most recent cases, a strategy designed to convince the examiner that we fully understand those cases and that the question itself is being addressed in a positive fashion.

The second issue which needs to be dealt with is the distinction which has been drawn between property damage and economic loss in the recent cases concerning defective premises and defective goods. The former is recoverable under the broad *Donoghue* v *Stevenson* principle, whereas the latter is recoverable only in exceptional cases, if at all. Reference needs to be made to the point made earlier in this chapter that, in respect of defective premises, the House of Lords in *Murphy* stated that such loss is to be regarded as pure economic loss. This effectively shuts the door on liability of a local authority for inadequate inspection of foundations, etc., at least in relation to the damage to the property itself. In order to deal effectively with this issue the student must convince the examiner that (s)he understands not only those points on which the distinction is clear, but also that (s)he appreciates the areas of uncertainty.

In the context of defective products, the drawing of the distinction between dangerous products and those which are safe but shoddy has resulted in the following position. Where the defective product causes personal injury or damage to property other than the product itself, that damage, together with any foreseeable losses consequential thereon, is actionable under *Donoghue* v *Stevenson* (above). On the other hand, where no such damage actually occurs, other equally foreseeable losses are treated as 'economic' and are irrecoverable except possibly in the special circumstances which we consider below. The losses so categorised include:

(a)   the price of the goods themselves, even where they are so defective as to be worthless, or any sum which represents their diminution in value;

(b)   the costs of repair even where that expenditure is incurred to obviate a dangerous defect in the goods, for a defect once discovered is no longer dangerous — see the *D & F Estates* case (above);

(c)   the loss of profits which would otherwise have been earned in the period awaiting the replacement of the defective product — see *Muirhead* v *Industrial Tank Specialities Ltd* [1985] 3 WLR 993.

Other losses are difficult to classify and the extent to which they are recoverable is somewhat uncertain. In *MIS Aswan Engineering Establishment Co.* v *Lupdine Ltd* [1987] 1 WLR 1, Lloyd LJ at p. 21 provides a number of very useful examples, perhaps the most important of which is the damage caused to the 'parent' product by a defective component. Does this constitute damage to other property so as to permit recovery under *Donoghue*? This difficulty was also recognised by Lord Bridge in the *D & F Estates* case (above), at p. 386, the point being expressly left open. A student who was able at this point to draw to the attention of the examiner, by way of comparison, the position where an action is brought under Part I of the Consumer Protection Act 1987, would undoubtedly be well rewarded. One other point which is worthy of mention in this context is the refusal of the House of Lords in *Lexmead (Basingstoke) Ltd* v *Lewis* [1982] AC 225 to treat restrictively, i.e., as economic loss, indemnity claims which arise by reason of personal injury; see also *The Kapetan Georges* [1988] FTLR 180. One interesting question upon which students could usefully ponder, is whether the *North Scottish Helicopter* case would now be decided differently in the light of the decision of the House of Lords in *D & F Estates* v *Church Commissioners* (above).

The fact that this latter decision has confirmed the distinction between dangerous and non-dangerous defects in the context of defective premises (with its attendant difficulties) would also need to be discussed. This could be achieved by explaining the close parallel which was drawn between defective products and defective premises in that case. It would also be necessary to explain that this originally only appeared to be so where the claim in respect of defective premises is brought against someone who is contractually involved in their construction, but now also includes situations where the claim is against, e.g., a local authority arising out of the alleged negligent exercise of statutory powers, the purpose of which is to ensure public safety.

The major part of the answer should be devoted to a discussion of the two lines of authority under which economic loss may be recovered and which we have previously identified, i.e., the *Hedley Byrne* principle and the now out of favour 'Wilberforce approach'.

Liability under the *Hedley Byrne* principle is well established and the boundaries are settled with some degree of certainty although *Caparo* may, as indicated earlier, have to be seen as a more restricting approach for the future. In order to ensure the relevance of their response to the question students should avoid regurgitating the case law explaining how the present position came about. What is required is a summary of that principle which outlines its major features, in particular those which demonstrate the limited scope of the principle. This would serve as a precursor to your discussion of the cases which fall outside it.

In defining the principle under *Hedley Byrne* the two most significant features which deserve particular attention are the need for the plaintiff to show detrimental reliance and the concept of a voluntary assumption of responsibility. With regard to the issue of reliance, students must be able to show that they appreciate the difference between the nature of detrimental reliance and what might be termed 'implied reliance'. Whilst this latter form of reliance is probably insufficient under *Hedley Byrne*, it would seem to be a factor of considerable importance in establishing the degree of proximity necessary to permit recovery under the 'Wilberforce approach'; see *Junior Books Ltd* v *Veitchi* [1982] 3 All ER 201 per Lords Fraser and Roskill at pp. 203 and 213, respectively although, see for example, Lord Keith in *Murphy* (referred to above).

In so far as the existence of the duty of care under *Hedley Byrne* is based upon a voluntary assumption of responsibility by the defendant, students need to show an awareness of the fact that such assumption is more often implied from the circumstances than it is expressed by the defendant himself. The point should be made that, in *Hedley Byrne* itself, the House of Lords took the view that an assumption of responsibility could not be implied on the grounds that the defendants had expressly disclaimed any such responsibility. In the words of Lord Devlin: 'A man cannot be said voluntarily to be undertaking a responsibility if at that very moment when he is said to be accepting it he declared that he in fact is not' [1964] AC 465 at 533.

In the previous edition we discussed the Court of Appeal decision in *Harris* v *Wyre DC*, which was subsequently reversed on appeal. The issue of voluntary assumption of responsibility lay at the heart of the case. The Court of Appeal had held that the defendant local authority owed no duty of care to the plaintiffs as prospective purchasers on the ground that the mortgage application form contained a disclaimer, the effect of which was to prevent the duty arising in the first place. Some members of the House of Lords took the view that the expression 'voluntary assumption of responsibility' was not a helpful or realistic test of liability and proceeded to approve of *Yianni* v *Edwin Evans & Sons* [1981] 3 All ER 592. A student might be expected to speculate about the relationship between *Harris* and the now apparent narrowing of liability as evidence in *Caparo*. There seems to be no hint of a suggestion that *Harris* was wrongly decided, and indeed the judges in *Caparo* seemed to approve of it.

The final part of any answer to our illustrative question requires a discussion of the extent to which economic loss is recoverable in circumstances which fall outside the *Hedley Byrne* principle. Given that the majority of recent decisions have been concerned with such claims, it would be necessary under examination conditions to summarise the collective effect of those cases in a fairly succinct fashion. In so doing students will need to demonstrate that they are aware of the expansionary trend brought about by the application of the 'Wilberforce approach', the peak of which was the decision in *Junior Books Ltd* v *Veitchi* (above), the first successful claim for economic loss in the House of Lords since *Hedley Byrne*.

Students would need to show not only an appreciation of the fact that this trend has been effectively ended, but also an understanding of how that has been achieved. In the earlier part of this chapter we highlighted a number of relevant points, e.g., the reinterpretation of the 'Wilberforce approach' by Lord Fraser in *Yuen Kun-yeu* v *Attorney General of Hong Kong* (above), so that a 'composite test' requiring much more than the mere foreseeability of harm, has to be satisfied before even a prima facie duty can be said to exist with regard to economic loss. In other cases, rather than indulge in close analysis of the degree of proximity as such, the courts have denied the existence of any duty of care on the broad ground that to impose such a duty would be neither fair nor reasonable. Furthermore, the courts have been seen to reaffirm the authority of precedent and to suggest that the 'Wilberforce approach' be confined to 'novel cases'. There are two other cases not so far mentioned which deserve to be raised in an answer at this particular point, namely *Simaan General Contracting Co* v *Pilkington Glass (No. 2)* [1988] 1 All ER 791 and *Greater Nottingham Co-op Society Ltd* v *Cementation Piling and Foundations Ltd* [1988] 3 WLR 396. In both these cases the earlier decision in *Junior Books* v *Veitchi* (above) was distinguished and in both cases the action for economic loss was unsuccessful. The importance of these decisions is that they demonstrate further the increasing isolation of the decision in *Junior Books* and really confirm the rejection of that decision as establishing any principle of general application under which the recovery of economic loss might be dealt with.

CONCLUSION

By way of a conclusion to an answer to the question, drawing together the main points expressed, it would be appropriate to point out that the cases in which plaintiffs have successfully recovered economic loss outside the *Hedley Byrne* principle are pretty thin on the ground. They obviously include *Junior Books* v *Veitchi* and those cases concerning the negligent survey/valuation of property, such as *Yianni* (above) and *Harris* (above). There are, in addition, the decisions in *Ross* v *Caunters* and *White* v *Jones* (above) and *Ministry of Housing and Local Government* v *Sharp* [1970] 2 WLR 802, CA and *Spring* v *Guardian Assurance plc* [1994] 3 WLR 354. We may also conclude that, given the policy considerations recognised earlier (concern to avoid indeterminate liability and the 'protection' of the established rules of contract law), the restrictions placed upon recovery which we identified in the case law will mean that it is likely that this list of authorities will be extended only in a cautious manner on a case by case basis. It seems that even the scope of the *Hedley Byrne* principle itself may be under attack (see *Caparo*).

SELECTED READING

Atiyah, 'Negligence and Economic Loss' (1967) 83 LQR 248.

Cane, 'Economic Loss in Tort: Is the Pendelum Out of Control' (1989) 52 MLR 200.

Craig, 'Negligent Misstatement, Negligent Acts and Economic Loss' (1976) 92 LQR 213.

Markesinis, 'An Expanding Tort Law — The Price of Rigid Contract Law' (1987) 103 LQR 359.

Stapleton, 'Duty of Care and Economic Loss: A Wider Agenda' (1991) 107 LQR 249.

10   NUISANCE AND THE RULE IN RYLANDS v FLETCHER

INTRODUCTION

In this chapter we propose to deal with both public and private nuisance and the rule in *Rylands* v *Fletcher* LR 3 HL 330, namely strict liability for the damage caused by the escape of 'dangerous things' from a person's land. These are three academically popular heads of liability selected from a number of different nominate and innominate torts which arise from the use or enjoyment of land. The possibility of liability under additional or alternative heads has to be borne in mind by the student. For example, trespass to land will give rise to a cause of action only where the interference with the land is of both a direct and physical nature, whereas nuisance extends to indirect substantial interferences of a physical or non-physical character such as smells and noise. We do not propose to discuss trespass to land, as there are very few examinable issues within its scope and this perhaps reflects its lack of emphasis in torts syllabuses generally. Nor do we propose to discuss various other specific sources of liability, such as those created by statute. These controls are not commonly taught in any meaningful way in a torts syllabus.

Any discussion of nuisance and *Rylands* v *Fletcher* ought, however, to take account of the enormous amount of development which has taken place in the tort of negligence this century. Account of that development must be taken for two reasons. First, the so-called strict liability in *Rylands* v *Fletcher* has fallen victim to the philosophy of no liability without fault. Secondly, negligence is a very important possible third head of liability in many situations concerned with the use or enjoyment of land. There exists a number of important distinctions between all three heads of liability which a student needs to appreciate. It is a particularly attractive area in which an examiner might set a question which crosses the boundaries of the three torts.

SUBSTANTIVE DIFFICULTIES

Nuisance

The first point which we would emphasise very strongly is that the whole of this area of law is riddled with detailed technicalities. The way the subject is approached by lecturers and tutors inevitably ignores large numbers of the technical issues in their efforts to deal with the general issues. There is always a great danger in an area such as this of over-simplification.

As we have indicated in the introduction we are not here concerned with the tort of trespass to land as such. Nevertheless the student needs to be aware of the technical distinctions between trespass and nuisance. Apart from the distinctions already mentioned above, there exist some important differences as to the nature of an interest in land which is protected by nuisance or trespass.

One of the most fundamental distinctions which students need to appreciate is that between private and public nuisance. Whilst there are certain issues common to both, for example, the notion of unreasonable interference (discussed below), and the rules concerning remoteness of damage, there exist numerous points of distinction. For example, in public nuisance there is no requirement that the plaintiff has an interest in land in the sense normally insisted upon in private nuisance. These differences will be developed further in the following discussion. The student should appreciate that public nuisance comprises a diverse range of conduct, for example, selling adulterated food, brothel-keeping, obstructing public highways. For our part we shall be confining consideration of public nuisance to those instances where the same facts may give rise to an action in both public and private nuisance.

The central concept in the law of nuisance is an *unreasonable interference* with the *reasonable* use and enjoyment of land. Students experience considerable difficulty in grasping the notion of unreasonable interference for a number of reasons. The first is that they commonly fail to state that the interference must be substantial. Secondly, they frequently fail to identify the relevant factors, such as the nature of the locality and the duration of the interference, which have been stated in the cases and also fail to give appropriate weight to those factors. This is particularly so given the distinction drawn between cases where there is physical damage to property and other cases where the interference is comprised of less tangible matters, for example, smells, noise etc. A third difficulty lies in the distinction between the notion of what is 'reasonable' in nuisance and that involved in negligence. It is quite clear that there are cases in which an action in nuisance will lie even though the defendant may well have exercised reasonable care. On the other hand, the case law clearly identifies a category of nuisance in which the plaintiff can only succeed where he can show a failure to take such care. It may appear from this that there are in a sense two identifiable categories of nuisance. However, there are those who are reluctant to accept such a proposition (see, for example, *Winfield and Jolowicz on Tort*, 13th ed., pp. 386-7), and we accept that if there are two categories as such, their respective boundaries are far from clear.

As we indicated above, the use to which the plaintiff has put his own land may be a consideration which has to be taken into account. To what extent can a plaintiff increase his neighbours responsibility by putting his own land to some extra-sensitive use? (See, for example, *Robinson* v *Kilvert* (1889) 41 ChD 88.)

There are a number of important distinctions between the respective principles of public and private nuisance which students either overlook or fail to appreciate sufficiently. First, whilst personal injuries and damage to personal property are actionable both in private and public nuisance, it appears that in private nuisance such an action is restricted to those persons with an interest in land. Secondly, in order to bring an action in public nuisance, the plaintiff must show special damage over and above that suffered by other members of the community.

If there is one issue which above all confuses students it is that of remoteness of damage in nuisance. In particular the decision in *The Wagon Mound (No. 2)* [1967] 1 AC 617 with its complex cross-appeals and its apparent contradiction of the earlier decision in *The Wagon Mound (No. 1)* [1961] AC 388 is a complete mystery to students.

There are a number of defences with which students fail to deal adequately in examination questions. The defence of statutory authority is important in practical terms. The difficulty with this defence is that its success or otherwise depends upon the interpretation of the wording of any particular statute. Consequently, it is not possible to say anything of a general nature about its effectiveness and it is difficult to examine in the context of a problem-type question. With regard to the defence of prescription, the student should remember two things. First, it does not apply at all to public nuisance. Secondly, the defendant must have been committing a continuous and actionable nuisance for the 20-year period for this defence to succeed. This second aspect is particularly important in view of the established rule that it is no defence to argue that the plaintiff came to the nuisance. For example, in *Sturges* v *Bridgman* (1879) 11 ChD 852 prior to the plaintiff extending his premises the court was of the opinion that the noise emanating from the defendant's premises was not sufficient to amount to an actionable nuisance. It only became such by virtue of the extension to the plaintiff's premises and it was no defence that the latter had come to the interference.

The recent decisions in *Miller* v *Jackson* [1977] QB 966, *Kennaway* v *Thompson* [1981] QB 88 and *Tetley* v *Chitty* [1986] 1 All ER 663 have highlighted the difficulty in deciding when it is or is not appropriate to award an injunction or indeed damages in lieu thereof. The novelty of some of the considerations accepted in certain judgments in these cases make it a popular issue for examiners to raise in examination questions.

The final issue on nuisance is the question — who can be sued? It may well be on the facts of any particular case that a number of parties are held jointly responsible. One area, the boundaries of which are uncertain, gives rise to a particular difficulty. In certain situations which are regarded as 'extra-hazardous', i.e., where there is a substantial probability of interference with use or enjoyment of property, an employer may find himself liable for a nuisance which is a result of the activities of an independent contractor.

Rylands v Fletcher

It is generally accepted today that there is unlikely to be any liability under this rule unless there is proof of fault of some kind on the part of the defendant. In short, the liability is no longer strict. Indeed, the House of Lords in the recent case of *Cambridge Water Co. Ltd* v *Eastern Counties Leather plc* [1994] 1 All ER 53 refused to impose strict liability in that it was held that the type of loss suffered by the plaintiff was not reasonably foreseeable. The undermining of the strict nature of the liability is accepted by students: what they often fail to understand is how this state of affairs has been reached. Both the scope and the nature of liability have been substantially altered through the decided cases by means of such concepts as common benefit and non-natural user. In addition the development of the various defences such as act of third parties, act of God and statutory authority has resulted in a situation in which it is difficult to see any advantage in suing under this rule as opposed to negligence. This, perhaps, explains the Law Commission's comment (Report No. 32, p. 7) that 'the rule in *Rylands* v *Fletcher*, by reason of its many limitations and exceptions, today seldom forms the basis of a successful claim in the courts'. Indeed, it is perhaps worth commenting that in the case of a personal injury claim it is safer for the plaintiff to rely on negligence rather than *Rylands* v *Fletcher*.

ILLUSTRATIVE PROBLEM

In 1979 a small housing development was constructed close to an industrial estate which had existed for 24 years. The factories on the estate were traditionally involved in various types of light engineering. In 1981 P purchased one of the houses which was closest to one of the factories on the estate occupied by D Ltd. In 1980 D Ltd, because of a slump in demand, had changed its line of business and began reprocessing chemical waste. The new business involved 24-hour working. Heavy delivery lorries had to use the road through the housing estate to gain access to D Ltd's factory. D's factory also emitted smells. Residents complained of being unable to sleep at night because of noise, and of nausea due to the smells. In 1984 there was a delivery of some particularly volatile chemical waste to D Ltd's factory, which required to be unloaded with extreme caution. Whilst the waste was being unloaded, as a result of a mistake by X, a self-employed delivery driver engaged by D Ltd to collect and deliver the waste, an explosion occurred. P's house was extensively damaged and his wife was seriously injured. The occupants of the housing estate were evacuated for several days, including Y, the proprietor of a local shop, whose business was affected.

Discuss possible liability in nuisance and under the rule in *Rylands* v *Fletcher*.

COMMENTARY

In the rubric to our question we have deliberately excluded discussion of the tort of negligence. There may well be liability under that head but what we are seeking to explore in the question is the extent to which, if at all, it might be advantageous to frame an action in nuisance or under the rule in *Rylands* v *Fletcher*. Even after exclusion of discussion of that head of liability, nevertheless the problem would be an extremely heavy one to cope with in an examination situation. As we have indicated at various points throughout this book, we regard the problem questions as exercises to be undertaken during term time. The problem we have chosen is a vehicle by means of which we are seeking to expose the distinctions between the various heads of liability. It is quite possible that an examiner might choose an essay-type question to explore these distinctions, for example, 'Compare and contrast liability in nuisance, *Rylands* v *Fletcher* and negligence'. When faced with a question of this type, it is important that the student selects and directs the material towards those distinctions, rather than to engage in what amounts to an attempt to regurgitate his or her notes on these topics. As far as a problem question in an examination is concerned, an examiner may well restrict discussion by means of the rubric more narrowly than we have done, for example, the student may be asked simply to discuss liability in nuisance. This should serve to reinforce the point that close attention should be paid to the rubric of each individual question.

Both the teaching and examination of this area of necessity ignore a substantial amount of public law, namely, various statutory provisions concerning planning and environmental controls. The student, even if aware of such controls, should reflect in his discussion the emphasis on the material actually covered in his lectures and seminars, which for our purposes in the main will be common law.

The student is faced immediately with a dilemma as to how to structure an answer to this problem, which, without doubt is somewhat convoluted. In the light of this we believe this presents a demanding exercise on the planning of an answer. The basic structure we shall adopt in this commentary is to deal with the potential liability arising first from the smells and noise and secondly, liability which might arise as a result of the explosion. The more detailed structure dealing with the order of the possible actions of the particular plaintiffs will emerge as the discussion progresses.

Liability for Smells and Noise

Claim under Rylands v Fletcher
The potential plaintiffs under this heading are the residents/owners on the small housing estate, thus giving rise to the possibility of some action in both private and public nuisance which will be considered shortly. However, on the facts it would be extremely doubtful whether any liability would arise in respect of noise and smells under the rule in *Rylands* v *Fletcher*. The essence of liability under this rule is an escape from land under the defendant's control of something which is likely to do mischief. Thus, so far as the noise made by the lorries is concerned there is no question of an escape and, therefore, no liability under the rule. As to the smells the rule has been held in the past to apply to an escape of noxious fumes (see, for example, *West* v *Bristol Tramways Co.* [1908] 2 KB 14). However, the modern reluctance to impose strict liability under the rule, may manifest itself in the rule being interpreted restrictively in these circumstances. A court might, therefore, accept the argument that the smells are not noxious and that their escape is not likely to do mischief. Alternatively, it should be recalled that in *Rylands* v *Fletcher* (1868) LR 3 HL 330, Lord Cairns LC (at pp. 338-40) imposed the requirement that use made by the defendant of his land had to be a 'non-natural user' for there to be liability under the rule. In the later case of *Rickards* v *Lothian* [1913] AC 263, Lord Moulton (at p. 280) giving judgment of the Privy Council stated:

> It must be some special use bringing with it increased danger to others, and must not merely be the ordinary use of land or such a use as is proper for the general benefit of the community.

This view of 'non-natural user' was endorsed by the House of Lords in *Read* v *J. Lyons & Co. Ltd* [1947] AC 156. As Lord Porter observed in that case the notion of 'non-natural user' will vary according to changing social circumstances. However, in the *Cambridge Water Co. Ltd* v *Eastern Counties Leather plc* case (above) Lord Goff stated (at p. 79) that the 'storage of substantial quantities of chemicals on industrial premises is an almost classic case of non-natural use even in an industrial complex'. On the facts of this problem the student should perhaps draw attention to the specific decision in *British Celanese Ltd* v *A. H. Hunt (Capacitors) Ltd* [1969] 1 WLR 959. Lawton J was not prepared to regard the storage of relatively innocuous strips of metal foil on an industrial estate as being a 'special use' bringing with it increased danger to others. In the light of this it is unlikely that escape of smells alone or even noise would give rise to liability under the rule. There are also other possible arguments against the imposition of liability under the rule, for example, the common benefit point referred to in Lord Moulton's dictum above. It is unlikely, however, following from Lord Goff's statement above, that the fact that the factory may benefit the local community, for example, by providing further and continuing employment opportunities, will of itself exclude the application of the rule.

Claims under private nuisance
The student might usefully begin by giving a clear statement as to what amounts to an actionable private nuisance. There must be an *unreasonable* interference with the reasonable use and enjoyment of land. Whilst on the facts of our problem no difficulty arises as to the reasonableness of the use and enjoyment by the residents of the housing estate, there is much to be said on the issue of the extent of the interference by the defendant. We referred earlier to the need for the student to concentrate on the advantage to be gained, if any, from pursuing an action in private nuisance as opposed to negligence. Perhaps the first point that should be made is that an action in private nuisance is confined to persons with an interest in the land affected. Even though personal injuries may be actionable, this limitation would appear to apply (see *Malone* v *Laskey* [1907] 2 KB 141). This requirement confines the action in private nuisance, hence people who may be affected by the smells and noise, but without a sufficient interest in land would have to sue in public nuisance or negligence.

So far as the possible action under private nuisance is concerned, we have to ask whether such an action would succeed where one in negligence would not. This concerns the consideration of the notion of the unreasonable interference and in particular whether it is necessary for the plaintiff to prove negligence in the narrow sense in order to succeed in private nuisance.

In order to go directly to this issue, a student could assume that there is a substantial interference, briefly drawing attention to the relevant factors such as its duration, the nature of the locality, the tangible nature of some of the harm and social utility. Relevant cases might include *Halsey* v *Esso Petroleum*

Co. Ltd [1961] 1 WLR 683, *Adams* v *Ursell* [1913] 1 Ch 269 and *St Helen's Smelting Co.* v *Tipping* (1865) 11 HL Cas 642. In those cases where the defendant himself has created a substantial interference of a continuing nature it would appear that he may be liable notwithstanding that he may have exercised reasonable care.

It would seem appropriate to consider next what, if any, defences might be open to the defendant on the facts of the problem. As the law stands at the moment it is no defence to say that the plaintiff came to the nuisance, even if D Ltd's activities did amount to an actionable nuisance prior to P's purchase of his house, see, for example, *Bliss* v *Hall* (1838) 4 Bing NC 183. The student might, however, draw attention to Lord Denning MR's dissenting judgment in *Miller* v *Jackson* [1977] QB 966 where he expressed in a forceful manner a contrary view. If the defence of prescription is to be made out by D Ltd they would be required to show that they have for 20 years or more continuously committed what amounts to an actionable nuisance. Assuming, on the facts, that smells and noise have only become a substantial interference since 1980, when D began reprocessing chemicals, then this defence is unlikely to be made out. The position is analogous to that in *Sturges* v *Bridgman* (1879) 11 ChD 852.

On the facts it may be that the remedy which the residents may regard as more important will be that of injunction rather than damages. Perhaps there are two particular points to be made about the injunction remedy. One is that since the court is concerned to prevent the plaintiff suffering from future interference, the court is not unduly concerned with the question of the defendant's blameworthiness, though that matter may affect the precise terms of the injunction itself. The second point is that it may be argued on the part of the defendants that damages ought to be granted in lieu of an injunction. In the light of the recent decisions in *Miller* v *Jackson* [1977] QB 966 and *Kennaway* v *Thompson* [1981] QB 88 it would perhaps be beneficial to discuss the circumstances in which it is considered appropriate to award damages in lieu. In *Shelfer* v *City of London Electric Lighting Co.* [1895] 1 Ch 287 the Court of Appeal expressed the view that the discretion should be exercised in cases where the nuisance was 'trivial and occasional'. The views of Cumming-Bruce LJ in *Miller* that no injunction should be granted against the defendant cricket club on the grounds of public interest and also that the plaintiff came to the nuisance, would seem to be inconsistent with the rule in *Shelfer*. It is hard to extract from *Miller* any true *ratio* on the injunction issue and this was clearly recognised by the Court of Appeal in *Kennaway* v *Thompson*. In this latter case the injunction granted against the defendants was in specific terms and not a complete ban on their activities. It may be that some similar order might be granted on the facts of our problem, for example, to restrict the deliveries to daytime hours, or to reduce the smell to more tolerable levels. In the event that this cannot be achieved, the result might well be an injunction which orders the cessation of chemical reprocessing at the premises, see, for example, *Bellew* v *Cement Ltd* [1948] IR 61; see also *Tetley* v *Chitty* [1986] 1 All ER 663, where McNeill J distinguished *Kennaway* v *Thompson* in deciding to grant a permanent and full injunction against the defendants, thus preventing the offending activity (go-karting) altogether.

Claims under public nuisance

We may begin this part of the answer by defining what amounts to public nuisance. It is constituted by an unreasonable interference or misuse which either affects the exercise of some public right or alternatively substantially affects the health, safety or convenience of a substantial number of people within the area of effect, see, for example, Denning LJ in *Attorney-General* v *PYA Quarries Ltd* [1957] 2 QB 169. On the facts it may be that the residents comprise a sufficiently substantial class to render the noise and smells a public nuisance, see *Halsey* v *Esso Petroleum Co. Ltd* [1961] 1 WLR 683. The advantages from the plaintiff's point of view of arguing a public nuisance has occurred are twofold. First, those people who do not have a sufficient interest in land to sue in private nuisance, may nevertheless sue in public nuisance, provided they can show special damage over and above that suffered by other members of the community generally, see, for example, *Rose* v *Miles* (1815) 4 M & S 101. Secondly, the action for the injunction to stop a public nuisance may be taken at the relation of the Attorney-General (a relator action), as in the *PYA Quarries* case, thus avoiding litigation costs falling on any individual in the event that the actions are unsuccessful.

Liability with Respect to the Explosion

This part of the question is concerned with the possibility of more specific claims by individuals and we have accordingly structured our discussion along the following lines:

    (a)   *P* v *D Ltd*.
    (b)   *P's wife* v *D Ltd*.
    (c)   *Y* v *D Ltd*.
    (d)   *Other residents* v *D Ltd*.

P v D Ltd

Before discussing the claims against D Ltd, it is essential to comment briefly upon the possible liability of X, the delivery driver. His liability will be dependent upon the principles of negligence discussed in previous chapters. In particular the student is referred to chapter 9 on the issue of whether X might be liable for Y's economic loss.

Returning to P's potential actions against D Ltd, there would appear to be on the face of it three possibilities: *Rylands* v *Fletcher*, private and public nuisance. The only advantage to P, given that he has suffered foreseeable damage to his property, in pursuing an action under one of the above heads as opposed to an action in negligence, would be if the liability was strict under the former. So far as an action in private nuisance is concerned and probably also public nuisance, where the interference is by way of isolated escape, it would appear that the plaintiff has to show a failure to take reasonable care. This appears to be true not only in those cases where the hazard has arisen either naturally or from the act of a third party (see *Leakey* v *National Trust* [1980] QB 485, *Sedleigh-Denfield* v *O'Callaghan* [1940] AC 880, and the recent case of *Home Brewery Co. Ltd* v *William Davis & Co. (Leicester) Ltd* [1987] 2 WLR 117), but also in those cases where the hazard is created by the defendant himself (see Thesiger in *SCM (United Kingdom) Ltd* v *W. J. Whittall & Son Ltd* [1970] 2 All ER 417 at p. 430). There is, however, one category of cases in which an employer may be liable in nuisance, either public or private, for the negligence of an independent contractor. These are cases in which there is a special danger of a nuisance being committed, see *Matania* v *National Provincial Bank Ltd* [1936] 2 All ER 633. Given the volatile nature of the chemical waste which gave rise to the explosion it may be that D Ltd might be liable on the grounds that it could be foreseen that a nuisance might occur. The student might query whether this is, indeed, a separate category from those mentioned already, for example, *Leakey* and *Sedleigh-Denfield*. There would seem to be little advantage on the facts of this problem in suing for damages alone in either private or public nuisance as opposed to negligence. However, if it is an injunction that is being sought then it seems to have been accepted by the Court of Appeal in *Miller* v *Jackson* [1977] QB 966 that the plaintiff must succeed in nuisance to be entitled to such an order.

As to defences it would be sufficient to note first that as regards public nuisance, prescription is no defence at all. So far as an action in private nuisance is concerned, since this is an isolated escape, the issue of that defence would not arise. Furthermore, in view of the type of damage caused to P the nature of the locality is immaterial to the question as to whether it is an actionable nuisance (see *St Helen's Smelting Co.* v *Tipping* (1865) 11 HL Cas 642). The final issue on nuisance is that since on the facts P's house is the only one to sustain actual damage, that would be sufficient to allow him to sue in public as well as private nuisance.

The remaining possible head under which P might claim is the rule in *Rylands* v *Fletcher*. We have already discussed in some detail the possibility that D Ltd's activities might be regarded as a natural use of land. Given that there is clearly an escape in the form of an explosion, the important point would appear to be whether it is a non-natural user in such circumstances. At first sight the volatile nature of the chemicals in question would seem to bring it within the category of 'things likely to do mischief' if they escape. Whilst in *Rainham Chemical Works Ltd v Belvedere Fish Guano Co.* [1921] 2 AC 465 it seems implicit that the manufacture of explosives amounts to a non-natural user, some members of the House of Lords in *Read v J. Lyons & Co. Ltd* [1947] AC 156 were reluctant to accept that a munitions factory in time of war would constitute a non-natural user. This must now be read in the light of Lord Goff's statement above in the *Cambridge Water* case. We would suggest that it is impossible to say with any degree of certainty whether or not the activity in the question would constitute a non-natural user. Whilst the decision in *British Celanese Ltd v A. H. Hunt (Capacitors) Ltd* [1969] 1 WLR 959 might be felt to be persuasive, it should be recognised, as we pointed out earlier, that the offending items in that case were fairly innocuous tin-foil strips.

The defence of act of a stranger would not appear to arise on the facts, since an independent contractor employed by a defendant, as in our problem, cannot be regarded as a stranger. Indeed, on the facts of *Rylands v Fletcher* itself the defendant was held liable for the negligence of his independent contractor (see also *Hale v Jennings Bros* [1938] 1 All ER 579).

As a conclusion to the discussion on *Rylands v Fletcher* the student might refer to the statement of Sellars LJ in *Dunne v North Western Gas Board* [1964] 2 QB 806 at p. 831 where he said that in the present time the defendant's liability under the rule in *Rylands v Fletcher* itself 'could simply have been placed on the defendant's failure of duty to take reasonable care'. However, Rees J in *Pearson v North Western Gas Board* [1968] 2 All ER 669, whilst applying the decision in *Dunne's* case doubted (at p. 672) whether the dictum by Sellars LJ would be accepted by the House of Lords. The editor of *Winfield* has been moved to comment, somewhat ironically, to the effect that the rule in *Rylands v Fletcher* is often unavailable at times when it is most needed, namely when the plaintiff cannot prove the defendant was at fault as in both *Dunne* and *Pearson.*

P's wife against D Ltd

As we have indicated earlier, an action in private nuisance for personal injuries may be possible provided the plaintiff has a sufficient interest in the land, see *Malone v Laskey* [1907] 2 KB 141, subject to the qualification in *Khorasandjian v Bush* (above). In the event that P's wife has no such interest in the house, then she will have to fall back upon the other possible causes of action. As for public nuisance, it is clearly established that personal injury damages are recoverable, and on the facts P's wife will have suffered special damage over and above that of the community in general. In the light of our earlier discussion, on the issue of fault it may be slightly easier to establish a case in public nuisance rather than negligence.

P's wife may, subject to what we said as to the availability of an action under *Rylands v Fletcher*, have a claim for personal injuries. However, it is not entirely free from doubt as to whether the rule in *Rylands* v *Fletcher* extends to personal injury damage. The only real doubt cast upon this prospect, is contained in a dictum of Lord Macmillan in *Read* v *J. Lyons & Co. Ltd* [1947] AC 156 (at p. 173) where he said that an allegation of negligence is essential in actions for personal injuries. As against that the student might refer to the earlier case of *Hale* v *Jennings Bros* [1938] 1 All ER 579, although there is a suggestion that some interest in land is a prerequisite of recovery. However, Parker LJ in *Perry* v *Kendricks Transport Ltd* [1956] 1 WLR 85 in expressing the view that liability under the rule did extend to personal injuries, appears to have anticipated no such limitation.

Y v D Ltd

The question arises here as to whether Y's loss, which appears to be pure economic loss as it is not consequential upon damage to his person or property, is recoverable. Even if an action in *Rylands* v *Fletcher* overcame the various hurdles we have discussed previously, there is considerable doubt whether the rule extends to recovery of pure economic loss. Widgery J in *Weller & Co.* v *Foot & Mouth Disease Research Institute* [1966] 1 QB 569 took the view that economic loss was no more actionable under *Rylands* v *Fletcher* than it was under the tort of negligence. That statement must now be reconsidered in the light of the developments which have taken place in negligence which we discussed particularly in chapter 9. So far as nuisance is concerned, however, the recovery of what may be termed pure economic loss' is recognised in decided cases on both public and private nuisance (see, for example, *Rose* v *Miles* (1815) 4 M & S 101 and *Benjamin* v *Storr* (1874) LR 9 CP 400 on public nuisance, *Fritz* v *Hobson* (1880) 14 ChD 542 and *Grosvenor Hotel Co.* v *Hamilton* [1894] 2 QB 836 on private nuisance). The losses sustained in this kind of case, though economic, are in one sense different from those sustained in other situations. They represent the result of an interference with a beneficial use or enjoyment of land even though no physical damage is done to the land in question. It is possible, therefore, that Y's claim is more likely to succeed under public or private nuisance rather than under *Rylands* v *Fletcher* and, moreover, negligence.

Other residents v D Ltd

The claims of these people relate to the expenses incurred in their necessary displacement from the dwellings. Under *Rylands* v *Fletcher* and indeed private nuisance there appears to be no reason in principle why such loss should not be recoverable, assuming that liability can be established under either head. Public nuisance is less attractive in this respect because of the requirement of special damage discussed above. Since all occupants of the estate have been evacuated it is arguable that the only person to have special damage are P, his wife and Y.

ILLUSTRATIVE QUESTION

Have a go at this one. Notice that the rubric deliberately excludes liability which might arise under the rule in *Rylands* v *Fletcher*.

D Ltd operates a large sawmill which has been established since 1956. The sawmill is situated in an area which was formerly industrial but which fell into dilapidation. In the 1980s the area underwent extensive redevelopment and is now essentially a residential area. In the past five years D Ltd's business has expanded considerably and now provides employment for over 100 local people.

There have been numerous complaints, particularly from residents occupying houses close to the sawmill. Residents have complained that their homes are constantly contaminated by sawdust blown from the waste heaps at the sawmill. They also claim that the large stockpiles of timber represent a serious fire risk to some homes which are only 30 metres away.

The sawmill now works on two shifts operating from 6.00 am to 10.00 pm. Despite the use by D Ltd of the best available technology to suppress noise, residents claim that the noise emitted from the sawwmill is stressful and disruptive.

In January 1994, during fierce gales, pieces of timber were blown from the stockpiles injuring people and causing damage to houses and cars standing in the highways.

Consider the possible liability of D Ltd in public and private nuisance.

SELECTED READING

Cane, 'Justice and Justification for Tort Liability' (1982) 2 OJLS 30, 51–61.

Dias, 'Trouble on Oiled Waters: Problems of Wagon Mound (No. 2)' [1967] CLJ 61.

Law Commission Report No. 32, 1970, *Civil Liability for Dangerous Things and Activities*.

McLaren, 'Nuisance Law and the Industrial Revolution' (1983) 3 OJLS 155.

Markesinis, 'Negligence, Nuisance and Affirmative Duties of Action' (1989) 105 LQR 104.

Ogus and Richardson, 'Economics and the Environment: A Study of Private Nuisance' [1977] CLJ 284.

Tromans, 'Nuisance, Prevention or Payment' [1982] CLJ 87.

Williams, 'Non-natural Use of Land' [1973] CLJ 310 Chapter 11.

11 INTERFERENCE WITH GOODS

INTRODUCTION

Prior to the Torts (Interference with Goods) Act 1977 a wrongful interference with goods might well have been actionable under any one or more of a number of torts, namely, trespass, conversion, detinue, replevin and indeed negligence. Each of these torts had its own rules which limited its application in terms of who could sue and be sued and what amounted to a 'wrongful interference'. In addition, defences were of variable application as indeed were the remedies open to the plaintiff. Apart from the vast array of technical distinctions, there existed a good degree of overlap, in particular between the torts of conversion and detinue. The opportunity to rationalise the position arose in 1971 with the publication of the Law Reform Committee's 18th Report, *Conversion and Detinue* (Cmnd 4774). However, the opportunity was spurned, and what resulted is, in effect, a half-hearted reform. Most of the changes are procedural in nature and a substantial number of the technical distinctions created at common law remain with us notwithstanding the 1977 Act. Had the recommendations of the Committee been fully implemented three different torts, namely trespass to goods, conversion and detinue would have been rationalised into a single tort of wrongful interference with goods. However, this was not the outcome and in order to determine whether any liability exists we still have to examine the common law with all its attendant difficulties. One small consolation is that detinue was abolished by the 1977 Act and those 'interferences' which detinue alone would remedy are now treated as acts of conversion.

Whilst this area does not generate a great deal of case law by comparison with the tort of negligence, it is nevertheless an area of some practical significance. Furthermore, the torts are conceptual in their nature and yet quite different from negligence. They introduce the student to property concepts such as ownership and possession and to the notion of relative title. For these reasons the area may well be represented in the sessional examination.

SUBSTANTIVE DIFFICULTIES

This is an area in which the basic principles and concepts themselves are not particularly well understood by students. The reason for this is perhaps that they are obscured to some extent by the technical distinctions referred to earlier. In particular, we have identified below those matters which in our experience give rise to the most difficulties.

Students find initial difficulty with the differences between trespass (*de bonis asportatis*) and conversion. The former is a tort which primarily protects *possession* rather than ownership, whereas conversion protects *ownership* rather than possession. From this stems a number of distinctions as to who can sue and who can be sued in these respective torts.

What amounts to a 'wrongful interference' for the purposes of an action in trespass is substantially different from that which is necessary in an action in conversion. As Lord Abinger pointed out in *Fouldes* v *Willoughby* (1841) 8 M & W 540 the mere act of removal of goods from the plaintiff's possession unaccompanied by any denial of the plaintiff's title to them, will not amount to conversion, although it might amount to trespass. The distinctions between the two torts are not of any great significance nowadays. What, however, remains of importance is whether a particular interference lies within the bounds of either trespass or conversion under the common law in order that it is recognised as wrongful. For example, V delivered goods to M by mistake. T's managing director offered to and did 'sell' the goods to M. It subsequently came to light that the goods were intended for another party. It was held that T was liable to V in conversion, that the actions of the managing director amounted to a sufficient denial of title. His dealing with the goods purported to dispose of ownership even though he did not physically handle them. The absence of this latter aspect meant that there was no trespass, but there was nonetheless a conversion (see *Van Oppen & Co. Ltd* v *Tredegars Ltd* (1921) 37 TLR 504). This serves to emphasise that the cases and principles which they embody remain of the utmost importance in drawing the line between actionable and non-actionable interferences.

The nature of the liability in both trespass and conversion is a source of considerable confusion to students. This is hardly surprising in view of the fact that they are told that these torts are, for example, categorised as 'intentional' torts in *Street on Torts* (9th ed.), and yet they are told that liability is strict. The explanation for this apparent conflict lies in the adjective 'intentional' being used to describe the act and not the defendant's state of mind *vis-à-vis* the consequences of that act. With regard to trespass (*de bonis asportatis*) and conversion it is sufficient that the act with regard to the goods is intentional. Thus, for example, a person who buys goods from a thief commits the tort of conversion notwithstanding that he honestly believes the thief to be the true owner (see, for example, *Cundy* v *Lindsay* (1878) 3 App Cas 459). Where, however, trespass takes the form of damaging goods, no action will lie if the defendant can prove that he had exercised reasonable care (see *National Coal Board* v *J. E. Evans & Co. (Cardiff) Ltd* [1951] 2 KB 861).

The references to the decision in *Cundy* v *Lindsay* reminds us that the law of torts is inextricably bound up with other areas of law, namely, the law of contract and the law of property. The basic rule governing the transfer of property is embodied in the maxim, *nemo dat quod non habet, a* person cannot pass a better title than he himself has. There are, however, numerous exceptions to this basic rule which operate to protect a bona fide purchaser from an action in conversion. Those contained in ss. 2, 8 and 9 of the Factors Act 1889 and ss. 23 to 25 of the Sale of Goods Act 1979 are all exclusively concerned with situations in which the person from whom the bona fide purchaser bought obtained possession of goods under an *apparently valid* contract but for some reason, for example, fraud, acquired only a defective title, or no title at all. We do not propose to discuss the detail of these provisions, as they are normally dealt with at some length in a commercial law or sale of goods syllabus (see chapter 6 of *SWOT Commercial and Consumer Law*). If, however, in your own syllabus this issue is dealt with in any depth, it would be wise to reflect the extent of that treatment in any answer, if appropriate, to an examination question.

There are in this area three specific issues which might well be regarded as highly examinable, namely, the position of the 'innocent improver', the issue of double liability and, finally, the law relating to finders. The 1977 Act deals with the first two, but the law relating to the latter is to be found solely in common law.

Taking these in turn, where a bona fide purchaser cannot bring himself within one of the exceptions to the *nemo dat* rule, he will be liable to an action in conversion. The question which arises is whether the owner is entitled to recover the goods from him without compensating the bona fide purchaser for any improvement made to those goods. The matter is now covered by s. 6 of the 1977 Act. There are sufficient points of interest which arise on the wording of this section to make it an examinable topic. In particular, what is an improvement? Is it subjectively or objectively assessed? Further, the improver must show that he acted in the mistaken but honest belief that he had good title to the goods in question. The issue dealt with by s. 6 must be distinguished from those situations where the value of the goods increases due to market fluctuation (see *BBMB Finance (Hong Kong)* v *EDA Holdings* [1990] 1 WLR 409, PC).

The issue of double liability is now dealt with by ss. 7 and 8 of the Act. The provision in s. 7 requires the court to avoid the imposition of double liability, but the procedures for achieving this are somewhat circuitous and do not rule out entirely the possibility of double liability.

Finally, it has been acknowledged that the old adage 'finding is keeping' is a dangerous half-truth. This is certainly the case given the convoluted state of the common law. The question of the finder's title depends very much upon the circumstances of the finding and affords an excellent illustration of the concept of relative possessory title.

ILLUSTRATIVE PROBLEM

O regularly leaves his van and trailer in the street with the ignition key and registration documents in the vehicle. The van and trailer are stolen by joy-riders who abandon them on D1's land. The van, found by a trespasser D2, is sold by the latter to D3. D3 spends £500 on repairing the damage caused by the joy-riders, and a further £200 having it sprayed in the colours of his local football club. The van is sold to D4. O has now traced the van to D4 and demands its return. D1 refuses to allow O to collect the trailer which was also left on his land. D1 lends it to D5 and it is destroyed in an accident. Discuss.

COMMENTARY

Notwithstanding that this is the final chapter we shall not eschew the opportunity of reminding students of the benefits of sketching out a rough plan of their answer. Whilst the structure of an answer to the above question logically falls into two parts, namely, liability arising with regard to (a) the van and (b) the trailer, each situation includes a number of parties and some forethought ought to be given as to the order of treatment.

Although the problem question does not directly ask 'How has the 1977 Act changed the common law', nevertheless the student should, where relevant, be at pains to demonstrate his or her knowledge as to what the common law was prior to the Act. However, the student should avoid writing an answer which is excessively devoted to a discussion of the pre-existing law.

Liability in Respect of the Van

A word of explanation is necessary as to the way in which we have chosen below to deal with the possible actions on the facts of the problem. We have adopted a pragmatic approach on the question as to whom O, and possibly D1, might sue. We deal briefly with the issue of the joy-riders, bearing in mind they are likely to be untraceable or not worth suing. Further, whilst in theory

O and D1 may bring actions against any one or all of D2, D3 and D4 it is most likely that D4 will be the person sued, in view of the fact that possession of the vehicle has been traced to him. Assuming that to be so, it is necessary to consider the possible claims in contract by D4 against D3 and in turn D3 against D2.

The joy-riders

In view of the practical difficulties to which we have already alluded, it would be sufficient for the student to make no more than brief observations on their potential liability. For example, they appear to have committed not only the tort of trespass and possibly conversion but also a criminal offence under s. 12 of the Theft Act 1968.

Interference by D2, D3 and D4

Against each or any of them an action may be brought by both O and D1. O's claim would obviously be based on his *proprietary* title to the goods. D1's claim, however, would be based upon a *possessory* title to the goods. If he has a better right to possession than any of D2, D3 or D4, then as against such wrongdoers he has a sufficient title to maintain an action. A person with a possessory title can maintain an action in either trespass or conversion against anyone except a person who can show a better title. This point is illustrated by the old case of *Armory v Delamirie* (1721) 1 Str 505 and, more recently, by the case of *Parker v British Airways Board* [1982] QB 1004. The plaintiff in this case found a gold bracelet on the floor of the executive lounge at Heathrow Airport, which he handed to the defendants in order that it might be returned to the true owner. He also left a note giving his name and address and asking that the bracelet be returned to him in the event that the owner failed to reclaim it. It was not reclaimed and the defendants sold the bracelet and retained the proceeds. After detailed consideration of the facts and the relevant case law, the Court of Appeal concluded that the plaintiff had the better right to possession than the Board and was therefore entitled to recover as damages the proceeds of sale. The question arises as to whether on the facts of the problem D1 has a better title to possession as against D2. It may be that the latter, in addition to being a trespasser on D1's land, commits an offence of theft by finding. Thus, by analogy with the decision in *Hibbert v McKiernan* [1948] 1 All ER 860, the probability is that D1 would be regarded as having the better right to possession. If this is so, then D2 may well be liable to D1 in both trespass and conversion. It would be trespass because there is a wrongful interference with goods, of which D1 had actual possession by virtue of the van being on his land at the time. Furthermore, the subsequent sale of the goods by D2 to D3 would be a wrongful dealing with goods amounting to denial of D1's title, albeit a possessory one.

The student should perhaps point out that any action by D1 against D3 or D4 could only be brought in conversion since at the time of their wrongful interference D1 had only a *right* to immediate possession, which is insufficient to found an action in trespass. Similarly, whilst any action by O against the joy-riders might be in either trespass or conversion, any action against D2, D3 or D4 would be one in conversion.

It should be pointed out that D3 and D4 may be liable in conversion, notwithstanding that they are bona fide purchasers for value without notice of the fact that their respective sellers had defective title. Their acts in relation to the goods are intentional acts which amount to a denial of the title of the true owner, O. The fact that neither intended the legal consequences is immaterial and in that sense liability is strict, see, for example, *Cundy* v *Lindsay* (1878) 3 App Cas 459. If, however, either can establish that some exception to the *nemo dat* rule applies, then they may acquire title and not be liable in conversion. The only exception which can apply here, given that the van was 'stolen', is that relating to market overt if the facts occurred before 3 January 1995 (see the Sale of Goods Amendment Act 1994). We shall assume for the purposes of further discussion that this exception has not been made out.

As we indicated at the outset any action brought by O would probably be brought against D4. This is equally true with regard to the possible action by D1. Thus we have the prospect of two claims, one based on a proprietary and the other based on a possessory title, against D4 each for the full value of the goods. The student should indicate in general terms that the possibility of 'double liability' did exist prior to the 1977 Act as a result of a number of established rules. First, a person with *only* a possessory title could recover the full value of the goods and there was normally no duty placed upon him to account over to the owner, if known. The restrictions on the defence of *jus tertii* prevented the defendant in many circumstances from defeating, for example, a finder's claim, on the grounds that a person other than the plaintiff (for example, the owner) had a better title or right to possession of the goods. Finally, in the event that the defendant satisfied judgment in favour of a plaintiff with possessory title only, he acquired only such title as that person had. Thus, if the true owner subsequently made a claim against him, he would be liable again for the full value of the goods. An illustration of this is to be found in the facts of *Wilson* v *Lombank Ltd* [1963] 1 WLR 1294. Had the defendant in that case not handed back the goods to the lawful owner he would have been open to an action in conversion, notwithstanding the fact that he had been held liable for the full value to a person with only a possessory title.

After the Act, on the facts of this particular case, in the event that D1 actually made a claim his action would be joined with that of O in the same proceedings, see s. 9, as would the respective contractual claims of D4 and D3. In such circumstances the relief awarded by the court 'shall be such as to avoid double liability of the wrongdoer' as between the claimants, see s. 7(2) of the Act. It appears from this that O, being the true owner, would be entitled to the full value and D1 would not be entitled to anything.

The second major issue involved here arises from the 'improvement' to the goods by D3. As we shall see the 1977 Act offers some protection to the honest improver and also any person who innocently purchases from him. First, however, we need to decide whether and the extent to which there has been any 'improvement' to the goods within the Act. The problem discloses two different aspects to this issue. The first is the question of the cost of the repairs to the vehicle. The expenditure of £500 by D3 on the repairs may not be an improvement of the condition of the goods in which they were *when O lost* possession. On the other hand, it can be seen that the expenditure has caused some measure of improvement of the vehicle's condition *in which it was received* by D3. The Act does not indicate what is meant by 'improvement'. However, one might use the decision in *Greenwood* v *Bennett* [1973] QB 195, as persuasive authority, that D3 has in fact effected an improvement in such circumstances within the meaning of the Act. D3 also spent £200 on respraying the vehicle in the colours of his local football team. The question arises as to whether this respraying of the vehicle, which we shall assume was not a necessary part of the repairs, amounts to an improvement. Whilst the Act again gives no guidance, the probable interpretation of 'improvement' will be to impose an objective test, namely, has it increased the market value of the goods? If on the evidence it has not, no allowance in favour of the innocent improver will be made for this expenditure.

In the event that the action would be brought against D3, then an allowance would be made as indicated above, provided he could show he had acted 'in the mistaken but honest belief that he had good title' to the goods, as provided in s. 6(1). On the facts of our problem, however, we have assumed that the action would be against D4. What is his position? Section 6(2) deals with this situation. A similar allowance will be made in favour of a purchaser in D4's position provided he can show that he acted in good faith. It is perhaps important to note that in this situation D4 will be required to show not only that *he* acted in good faith, but also that D3 acted in the mistaken but honest belief that he (D3) had good title to the goods. The requirements in s. 6(1) and (2) would appear to be cumulative and not alternative. In the event that D3 did not act in the mistaken but honest belief that he had good title, then no allowance for improvement will be made in favour of the subsequent purchaser (D4), even though in good faith. O would, therefore, be able to recover the vehicle itself or its value as repaired. This may seem somewhat unfair to D4, bearing in mind his good faith. However, D4 has a contractual claim against D3 for the full price paid (see Sale of Goods Act 1979, s. 12, and *Rowland* v *Divall* [1923] 2 KB 500) and s. 6(3) of the 1977 Act will not apply, given that D3 does not act in good faith.

Assuming, however, that D4 can satisfy the terms of both s. 6(1) and s. 6(2), then he would be entitled to an allowance for the value of any improvements as against O. Such an allowance would also be made under s. 6(3) in an action, if any, by D4 against D3, thus preventing unjust enrichment of D4 at the expense of D3.

To finish this first part of the problem concerning the van, it is perhaps worth mentioning that D3 would have a contractual action against D2, but it would be limited to the price paid by him to D2 (see Sale of Goods Act 1979, s. 12). The student should perhaps point out that the defence of contributory negligence deliberately suggested by the facts, namely, leaving the car unattended with keys in the ignition etc., would not be open to D2, D3 or D4 if sued by O. This is clearly the position by virtue of s. 11 of the 1977 Act which provides that the defence is not applicable in proceedings 'founded on conversion, or on intentional trespass to goods'.

Liability in Respect of the Trailer

D1 would incur no liability towards O merely by his possession of the trailer when it was abandoned on his land. He is in fact an involuntary bailee. However, he may become liable to O as a result of denying O access to recover it. Denial of access to goods may amount to a conversion of them, provided it can be shown that there is sufficient denial, accompanied by some form of dealing with the goods. Since D1 is in possession his retention of possession would amount to a dealing or handling of the goods and in the light of the recent decision of *Howard E. Perry & Co. Ltd* v *British Railways Board* [1980] 1 WLR 1375 may well be treated as a sufficient denial of title to constitute conversion. The defendants who were experiencing an industrial dispute amongst their employees, in order to avoid aggravating the situation, refused to allow collection of goods from their depots. In an action brought by the plaintiffs Sir Robert Megarry V-C (at p. 1380) took the view that the refusal to deliver up the goods was 'a clear case of conversion'. His lordship was at pains to emphasise that the defendants were effectively denying most rights of ownership including the right to possession for an indefinite period of time. In so far as D1 has made no qualification upon his refusal to grant access in terms of when and how O may be allowed to retake possession, then there may well be a conversion.

Even if this were not the case, then D1's action in lending the trailer to D5 and the latter's user would render them both liable in conversion to O. If D5 alone were sued in conversion by O, it is clear from the facts of the problem that D5 would have no contractual claim against D1. However, he would presumably seek to bring D1 into the action as a joint tortfeasor under the provisions of the Civil Liability (Contribution) Act 1978 and thus endeavour to obtain a contribution from D1 as a joint tortfeasor. We have already emphasised that D5's innocence or good faith will not avail him of any defence. Nor would he be able to rely on any of the exceptions to the *nemo dat* rule.

ILLUSTRATIVE QUESTION

Try this one. There is a little contract law mixed in for good measure.

Albert hires a number of theatrical costumes from Beltadress Ltd and stores them in a local hall where a play is to be performed. A thief steals them from an unlocked cupboard but discards them in a field owned by Glum, a farmer.

Glum uses one of the costumes on a scarecrow and gives the other to his wife Buttercup who wears it for the Rag Ball at the local university. Buttercup then sells the costume to her friend Helen who spends £30 having the costume altered to fit her diminutive figure. Beltadress Ltd has now traced the costumes and demands their return.

Explain the legal position of the various parties.

SELECTED READING

Burnett, 'Conversion by an Involuntary Bailee' (1960) 76 LQR 364.

Law Reform Committee, 18th Report, *Conversion and Detinue*, 1971, Cmnd 4774.

Palmer, 'The Application of the Torts (Interference with Goods) Act 1977 to Actions in Bailment' (1978) 41 MLR 629.

BIBLIOGRAPHY

Atiyah/Cane, *Accidents, Compensation and the Law*, 5th edn, London: Butterworths, 1993.

Buckley, R., *Modern Law of Negligence*, 2nd edn, London: Butterworths, 1993.

Cane, P., *Tort Law and Economic Interests*, Oxford: Oxford University Press, 1991.

Clerk and Lindsell, *Torts*, 16th edn, London: Sweet & Maxwell, 1989.

Fleming, J., *The Law of Torts*, 8th edn, London: Sweet & Maxwell, 1993.

Hepple and Matthews, *Tort: Cases and Materials*, 4th edn, London: Butterworths, 1991.

Jones, M., *Textbook on Torts*, 4th edn, London: Blackstone Press, 1993.

Markesinis and Deakin, *Tort Law*, 3rd edn, Oxford: Oxford University Press, 1994.

Mullany and Handford, *Tort Liability for Pyschiatric Damage*, Australia: The Law Book Company Ltd, 1993.

Salmond and Heuston, *The Law of Tort*, 20th edn, London: Sweet & Maxwell, 1992.

Street, *On Torts* (ed Brazier), 9th edn, London: Butterworths, 1993.

Weir, T., *A Casebook on Tort*, 7th edn, London: Sweet & Maxwell, 1992.

Winfield and Jolowicz, *On Tort*, 14th edn, London: Sweet & Maxwell, 1994.

INDEX

TITLE IN THE SERIES

SWOT Constitutional and Administrative Law
SWOT Law of Evidence
SWOT Company Law
SWOT Law of Contract
SWOT Family Law
SWOT Land Law
SWOT Criminal Law
SWOT Equity and Trusts
SWOT Commercial and Consumer Law
SWOT A Level Law
SWOT Law of Torts
SWOT Jurisprudence
SWOT Employment Law
SWOT English Legal System
SWOT EC Law
SWOT Conveyancing
SWOT Law of Succession
SWOT Intellectual Property Law